Flexography Primer

Second Edition

by J. Page Crouch

GATFPress
Pittsburgh

International Standard Book Number: 0-88362-204-1
Library of Congress Catalog Card Number: 97-74132

Printed in the United States of America
Catalog No. 13302
Second Edition
First printing, September 1998
Second printing, July 2000

 Printed on Williamsburg Offset Smooth Finish, 60-lb. Paper
from Union Camp in Franklin, Virginia

GATF*Press* books are widely used by companies, associations, and schools for
training, marketing, and resale. Quantity discounts are available by contacting
Peter Oresick at 800/910-GATF.

GATF*Press*   **Orders to:**
Graphic Arts Technical Foundation   GATF Orders
200 Deer Run Road   P.O. Box 1020
Sewickley, PA 15143-2600   Sewickley, PA 15143-1020
Phone: 412/741-6860   Phone (U.S. and Canada): 800/662-3916
Fax: 412/741-2311   Phone (all other countries): 412/741-5733
Email: info@gatf.org   Fax: 412/741-0609
Internet: http://www.gatf.org   Email: gatforders@abdintl.com

TABLE OF CONTENTS

FOREWORD

A crash course in flexographic printing? Yes, that's what we have asked of J. Page Crouch, Alumni Distinguished Professor of Graphic Communications at Clemson University. This book offers a short, illustrated, non-technical orientation to the field along with a glossary of basic terms.

The aim of the GATF*Press* primer series is to communicate the essential concepts of printing processes and technologies. Other primers focus on lithography, gravure, and screen printing, and new titles are being planned.

Flexography Primer is useful to students, graphic artists, print buyers, publishers, salespeople in the graphic communications industry—to anyone who would like to know more about the printing process.

GATF*Press* is committed to serving the graphic communications community as a leading publisher of technical information. Please visit the GATF website at www.gatf.org for additional information about our resources and services.

Peter Oresick
Director
GATF*Press*

This book is dedicated to my father, with Mom in hand. As a lifelong teacher and author of several very successful books, he encouraged me to write and provided a model for me to follow.

PREFACE

Flexography is a printing process that has come of age. Named for the flexible plates it employs, flexo provides outstanding quality and superior performance for many printing applications. It is especially popular today in the packaging industry and enjoys expanding market opportunities.

This book is intended for educators, students, graphic artists, marketing professionals, customers, and others who need a fundamental background in this printing process. This book presents all of the concepts, vocabulary, technologies, trade practices, workflows, and current applications associated with flexography. I have used diagrams, charts, and photographs liberally to clarify the text, and a glossary to aid in more accurate communication.

As a student of printing, I clearly owe much to my many teachers. These include many fellow faculty members and literally hundreds of friends in the industries. I especially want to recognize George Oswald, my first flexo teacher, whose inspiring presentation to a group of Clemson students almost thirty years ago launched me into flexo education. Thanks also to Mark Andrews, Sr. (namesake of Mark Andy, Inc.) for his gift of a 2-in., one-color web press, and Jim Smith (founder of Tag & Label Corp.) for teaching me what to do with it. Finally, thanks to my hundreds of students with thousands of questions that prepared me for this project.

I hope this book is a testament to the diversity, complexity, technology, and production quality of today's industry.

J. Page Crouch
Clemson University
July 1998

1 THE PRINTING PROCESSES

Before one can understand the distinctions between and competition among printing processes, a clear understanding of their core concepts is needed. The key to the rest of the story is the principle applied to separate the image from the nonimage areas in each process. This is where we will begin.

THE PROCESSES

LETTERPRESS

Letterpress, the original printing method, is a *relief* process. The printing plate is hard; it has a reverse-reading image raised above the nonimage area. When rollers carrying an even and thin coat of paste ink are rolled over the surface, the only part of the plate to receive ink is the raised "face" of the image. This inked image is immediately impressed against the substrate (the material being printed), creating a right-reading reproduction. Figure 1-1 illustrates the plate and the way it transfers ink to a substrate.

The hard letterpress plate is either made of metal, usually magnesium, or photopolymer. Modern applications are most commonly on web (roll)-fed presses where the plate is wrapped around a cylinder. Letterpress requires a roller train, to work the heavy paste ink into a semi-liquid, uniform film for transfer to the plate. Figure 1-1 shows the flow of ink over the roller train to the plate. This roller train system has many moving parts and requires proper adjustment and maintenance to perform at a high-quality level. Because the plate is hard, it only produces high quality on very smooth surfaces. Thus it is not very useful for many porous, irregular substrates.

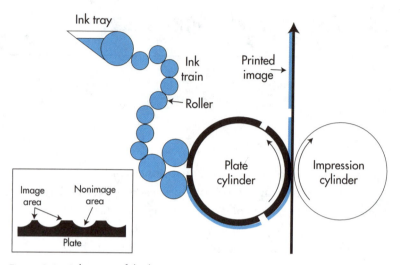

Figure 1-1. Schematic of the letterpress printing process.

Narrow-web letterpresses, the ones most commonly found in competition with flexo, use ultraviolet (UV) curing inks in order to achieve any reasonable production speed. These require expensive curing units on each print unit. This makes letterpress an expensive alternative, still limited to the smoothest of substrates, when compared to flexography. It is estimated that 7%* of printing is currently done by letterpress.

LITHOGRAPHY

Offset lithography is the leading process (estimated to be 46%) in total dollar volume of printing and dominates general commercial printing markets. The plate is flat and the image area is separated from nonimages by its chemical difference. The right-reading image area is water repellent while the nonimage area is receptive to water. Figure 1-2 illustrates the image and nonimage areas of the plate. The press requires two roller trains: a short one that coats the plate with a very thin layer of acidic water and a second one, much the same as letterpress, to deliver a thin film of ink. When the dampening (water) system wets the plate, the water-repellent image

* Statistics for print market shares taken from Mike Bruno's *What's New(s) in Graphic Communications*, No. 129 (July–August 1997)

Figure 1-2. Image and nonimage areas of the offset lithographic plate.

sheds the moisture, thus remaining dry. The plate is then contacted
with the inked rollers. Ink rollers transfer the ink to the dry images,
while the wet nonimage areas repel the ink. This is the principle of
lithography.

The process is called *offset lithography* because it prints first onto
a rubber surface called a *blanket* where the now-reverse-reading
inked image remains wet long enough to transfer, offset, onto the
substrate. It is really a misnomer to call the process "offset" printing
since the offset principle is also often applied to letterpress and
gravure. Figure 1-3 diagrams the offset lithographic printing unit.

Dry offset (another misnomer) is also based on a chemical principle where the image area is ink receptive and the nonimage area is
ink repellent. This is generally considered an improvement over
lithography since it eliminates the need for water and the entire
dampening system. It employs a very-high-tack (sticky) ink that will
not transfer to the nonimage area, which is silicone coated. The
printing unit is the same as conventional lithography without a
dampening system. It does, however, have to be temperature-
controlled due to the heat generated by the very tacky inks.

Conventional lithographic plates are inexpensive in comparison
to all other printing processes and thus affordable for even the
shortest of production runs. The plates are exposed and processed

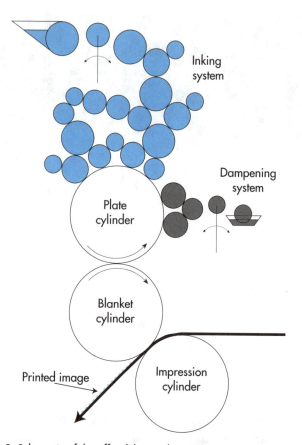

Figure 1-3. Schematic of the offset lithographic printing unit.

on inexpensive machines, which further explains the popularity of this process for the general commercial industry that is dominated by small local entrepreneurships.

GRAVURE

Gravure printing is perhaps the simplest printing process, employing a precision metal cylinder with image areas composed of tiny cells cut into the metal surface. This cylinder is simply rotated in a pan of ink and its nonimage surface is wiped (doctored) with a very thin metal, plastic or other synthetic composition blade called a doctor blade. The doctor blade wipes the smooth surface clean of ink leaving the image areas (cells) filled with ink, which transfers when impressed against the substrate.

Figure 1-4 illustrates the gravure image carrier. There is only one moving part. Since it is a "direct" process, meaning the imaged plate prints directly to the substrate, it requires a smooth receiving surface that contacts all the cells or there will be voids in the image, sometimes described as snowflakes. Unfortunately, there is always a downside. The imaging process actually cuts the cells into the cylinder, usually copper. This means that making a new "plate" requires cutting off the old image, replacing the metal surface, and re-imaging the new job. This is costly and time consuming. If it were not for the cost of cylinders, this process would be a producer of far more than its current market share of approximately 18% of all print. The limitation of gravure to smooth substrates can be eliminated by printing onto an offset blanket which, in turn, can be impressed onto the widest assortment of surfaces. There are, of course, technical issues to contend with all scenarios.

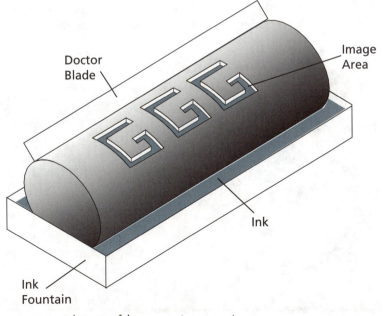

Figure 1-4. Schematic of the gravure image carrier.

SCREEN PRINTING

Screen printing, still known by too many as "silk screening," is a stencil process, wherein the image area is open and the nonimage area is closed. Ink is moved through the stencil by a resilient squeegee. The stencil/plate is made from a light-sensitive emulsion, photographically imaged so the areas to print are washed away while the nonimage areas are made permanent. The stencil is processed on a fine mesh, most commonly polyester, which holds the parts of the design in place. Without the screen mesh there would be a problem holding the centers of letters such as D, P, and A in position. Ink is transferred through the open stencil and mesh onto the substrate. Figure 1-5 labels the parts of the screen printing system.

Screen printing permits the control of ink film thickness by the diameter of the fibers that form the mesh. It is capable of applying very thick ink films, a strength. It is, however, limited in how thin a film of ink it can produce. It is widely used in the highest quality of packaging labels and in outdoor advertising where qualities including long life and continuous resistance to the elements are required. Its thick ink film provides more pigment deposit, which facilitates

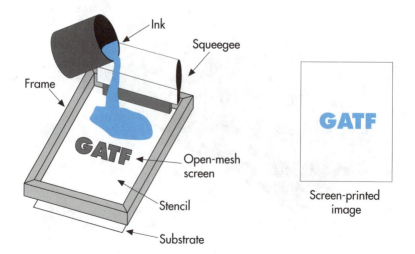

Figure 1-5. Schematic of the screen printing process.

great durability. It is routinely found in both flatbed and rotary applications. It is commonly used in-line with other processes where its thick ink film is desired for visual and/or tactile appeal or for protection, as in applications of clear coatings over other printing.

Screen printing accounts for an estimated 3% ($41.4–$68.1 billion) of graphics printing. Screen printing is also a major industrial process used in imaging dials and gauges; production of gaskets; glass, ceramic, and metal decoration; and electrical and electronic switches, circuits, and component manufacturing.

FLEXOGRAPHY

Flexography, the subject of this book, is a relief process similar to letterpress. Relief, however, is where the similarities end. The flexo plate is resilient instead of hard like letterpress. The flexographic ink is a liquid instead of paste. And the inking system is simple; it is a gravure cylinder called an *anilox roll*. The anilox roll is inked, wiped clean (usually with a doctor blade), and transferred onto the raised image area of the resilient plate. The ink remains wet long enough to transfer to the substrate. Because the plate is resilient, made of rubber or photopolymer, it can be impressed against the widest variety of surfaces and print without voids,

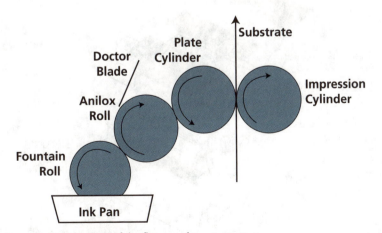

Figure 1-6. Schematic of the flexographic print station.

snowflakes. Approximately 18% of printing is produced by the flexographic process. Figure 1-6 provides a diagram of the simple flexo print station.

DIGITAL PRINTING

Digital printing, the youngest of all approaches, is most commonly an application of electrostatics whereby image and nonimage areas are separated by their electrical charge or polarity. The image is positively charged. It attracts negatively charged ink or pigment particles. These are transferred to substrates and fused for adhesion. Colorants may be liquid or powder, and image transfer may be direct to substrate or offset from an intermediate blanket. At the time of writing, digital printing was in rapid development with new markets being seen continuously. Variable imaging of each impression permits personalization and a spectrum of new possibilities for creative solutions not available from traditional printing methods. Digital printing is commonly installed in-line with other methods for its unique capabilities.

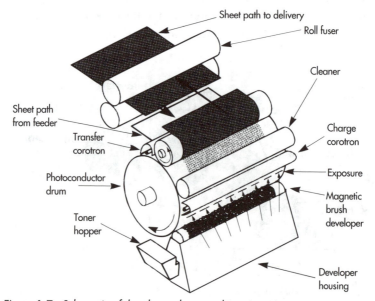

Figure 1-7. Schematic of the electrophotographic print unit.

Comparison chart of the major printing processes

Attributes	Rotary Letterpress	Offset	Gravure	Screen	Flexography	Digital
Ink Type	UV paste	Paste	Liquid	Viscous fluid	Liquid	Liquid or dry powder
Inking System	Roller train/complex	Roller train/complex	Very simple	Very simple	Anilox/simple	Simple
Image/Nonimage	Hard raised image	Flat/water repellent image	Recessed image	Porous/open image	Raised resilient image	No plate/image polarity
Repeat	Variable	Fixed	Variable	Variable	Variable	Fixed
Prep Costs	High	Low	Very high	Low to medium	High	Low
Image Transfer	Direct	Indirect/offset	Direct/can be offset	Direct	Direct	Direct and offset
Direct-to-Plate Option	No	Yes	Yes	Yes	Yes	NA
Substrate Versatility	Limited	Excellent	Limited unless offset	Excellent	Excellent	Limited

2 INTRODUCTION TO FLEXOGRAPHY

Flexography has its origins in the development of natural and synthetic rubbers. Natural rubber is obtained by the treatment of latex, a milky exudation of various trees and plants primarily native to the tropics. It was used by many pre-Columbian civilizations in Central and South America (such as the Mayas). Samples of rubber were sent back to Europe by missionaries and explorers in the sixteenth century, and in the late eighteenth century British chemist Joseph Priestley (famous primarily as the discoverer of oxygen) found that latex rubber, when heated, would erase pencil marks. From this "rubbing" ability, he coined the term "rubber."

In 1839 Charles Goodyear accidentally discovered a means of strengthening natural rubber, a process he called "vulcanization." In the mid- to late 1800s, various rubber products and patents began appearing.

In the late 1800s letterpress (printing from raised type, typically bits of metal) was the dominant form of printing, with the alternate processes of lithography and gravure still in their formative years. It was found that letterpress type could be set into plaster and that unvulcanized liquid rubber could be poured into the mold and, after heating and cooling, could make a workable rubber stamp. Soon, it was found that the rubber stamp concept could be applied to the manufacture of printing plates, which could be useful for printing on surfaces that did not yield good results with conventional letterpress processes, in particular corrugated paperboard.

The invention in the 1930s of synthetic rubbers made the properties of the rubber stamps and plates much more reliable than they were with unreliable natural rubber. Advances in rubber platemaking were pioneered by the Mosstype Corporation, which developed effective processes for both aniline printing (as flexography was known until the 1950s) and for letterpress printing. In the 1940s, Mosstype developed effective off-press plate-mounting systems, which minimized downtime and made aniline printing more efficient. In 1938, two men at the International Printing Ink Corporation devised a way of accurately and effectively metering the film of ink transferred to the rubber plate. Their system was inspired by the etching of gravure cylinders, which transfers ink from cells to the substrate. They developed an ink roller, engraved with a controlled size and number of cells, and plated with copper and chrome that effectively metered the ink film transferred to the aniline printing plate. They called their roller an anilox roller, and it is still the basis of modern flexographic presses.

In the first decades of the twentieth century, as was mentioned, flexography was known as "aniline printing," taking its name from the type of dyestuff used in the inks. In the 1930s, the aniline dyes were declared toxic by the FDA. Although aniline printers were by then using different types of inks, the name remained. In the late '40s, it grew apparent to industry leaders that the name "aniline printing" had to go, as the name had bad connotations, since the process was widely used for printing food packaging. In 1951, the Mosstype Corporation, in its company newsletter, held a contest to rename the process. Alternate names were solicited, and a final choice would be voted on. Two hundred suggestions came in from printers around the country, and a special committee formed by the Packaging Institute pared the list down to three: permatone process, rotopake process, and flexographic process. On October 21, 1952, it was announced that the overwhelming choice was "flexographic process," or "flexography."

FLEXOGRAPHY'S STRENGTHS

VARIABLE REPEAT
The term "repeat" refers to the length of one revolution of the plate cylinder. In offset lithography the repeat length is fixed. This means

that when one purchases a printing press, the size of the plate cylinder cannot be changed and it takes only one size of plate. Specialized applications have cylinders sized to fit the standard products the press was purchased to print. Since the size of the flexographic plate cylinder is variable on a press, any number of different-sized print jobs can be run with minimal waste, as can be seen in Figure 2-1.

Packaging, labels, and paperboard cartons, however, are specified in any size desired for the application. This means that full utilization of a web is only possible if the plate cylinder can be custom-sized to the specific job being run. Most flexographic presses are designed to permit "variable repeat" plate cylinders. Figure 2-2 shows how the anilox roll moves in and out to make room for a wide range of cylinder diameters. Exceptions to this are found in the presses that print directly on corrugated board for packaging and displays, and on sheetfed presses made to print envelope blanks.

Variable-repeat web presses permit optimizing production for the specific job and make flexography and gravure very competitive over offset lithography in many markets, especially where run lengths are long.

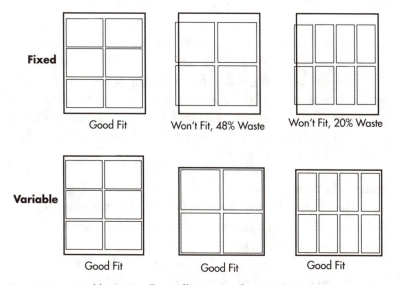

Figure 2-1. *Variable repeat allows efficient use of printing resources.*

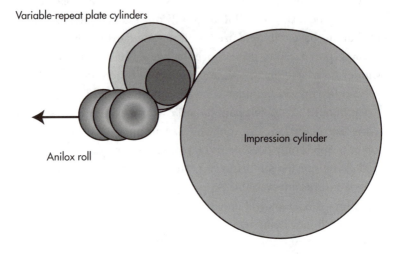

Figure 2-2. *The anilox roll moves in and out to make room for a wide range of plate cylinder diameters.*

RESILIENT PLATE

The flexographic plate is manufactured to an assortment of desired hardnesses depending on the application. In concept, if the substrate is irregular, it is desirable to use a plate that will be soft enough to conform to the irregularities, thus achieving full impression and printing that is free of voids. The most extreme example might be printing on corrugated board with a rather washboard surface. A soft plate, 25–40 durometer, will give enough to conform to this surface without crushing the corrugated structure. On the other hand, a different substrate would not need such a soft plate and would print sharper with one of a harder durometer, possibly 55–60 durometer.

ANILOX INKING SYSTEM

The anilox roll, which may be thought of as a gravure cylinder, controls the quantity of ink delivered to the plate. On soft, absorbent paper a relatively large quantity of ink will be required to fill the pores and provide uniform density. On nonabsorbent film or foil substrates all the ink will sit on top of the surface. This application requires an anilox roll with smaller cells so that relatively little ink is deposited onto the substrate. Excess ink film thickness results in images spreading, creating a halo around the edges and causing excessive dot gain or darkening in reproductions of photographs. Most modern flexographic presses permit fast changing of anilox rolls, which enables the printer to adapt the press for the specific application at hand. Chapter 5 will go into more detail on the language and current technology of anilox rolls. Figure 2-3 shows how cell size varies to determine the amount of ink to be printed.

Liquid Fast-Drying Inks

Flexography uses liquid inks that can be dried very quickly, permitting good production speeds. When combined with anilox inking, the process is capable of excellent consistency throughout production runs and good repeatability on repeat orders of the same job. Flexo inks may be solvent based, water reducible, or ultraviolet (UV) cured. Chapter 5 will discuss the common ink systems and the variety of demands placed on the process by the multitude of applications served by the flexographic process.

Configurations for In-Line Converting

Flexography is the leading printing method used by the converting industries. *Converting* is any finishing operation that forms a material into another physical form. Bagmaking, boxmaking, bookbinding, waxing, coating, laminating, folding, gluing, diecutting, etc., are all considered converting operations. Envelope converters make rolls of plain paper into stacks of printed and finished envelopes, all at one time on the same production line. They just happen to print images as part of that production process. This means that many of the flexographic printing machines are part of the in-line converting process. These same machines are capable of converting a wide variety of products, which is not as common with most other printing processes. Therefore, flexo printing has become the favored method often because its in-line converting capability is so productive.

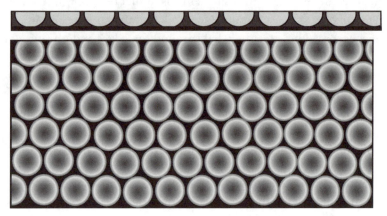

Above: More cells per inch of a given depth compared to fewer, deeper cells below. The anilox below carries more ink than the one at the top. More ink volume will cover rough, absorbent substrate, but will provide too much ink for fine screens and detail.

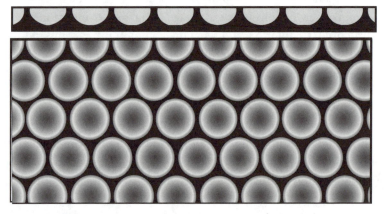

Figure 2-3. Cell size varies to determine the amount of ink to be printed.

Because today flexography is capable of excellent print quality, its in-line converting capacity allows it to be more competitive for such things as folding carton production, normally done on expensive sheetfed offset presses. Large amounts of space are required to let the sheets sit while ink dries before the sheets can be diecut. The platen diecutters are also very expensive and space consuming

compared to the rotary diecutting stations built in to the converting sections of flexo web presses.

FLEXOGRAPHY'S WEAKNESSES

The resilient plate, previously mentioned as a strength of flexography, has also tarnished the reputation of flexography's print quality.
In gravure printing, if there is a flaw in the cylinder it must be
repaired or reimaged. In lithography a flawed plate or blanket is
replaced. In flexography, however, the plate with a low spot is too
often impressed more so the low spot will print. The result is excess
squeeze, causing excess dot gain in all the areas except the low part
of the plate, which now looks fine.

   Another weakness is the tendency to apply a "one anilox fits all"
approach to production on a variety of substrates. The amount of
ink needed for quality printing is determined by the surface properties of the material being printed. When a single anilox roll is
used, it must be able to produce density and good coverage on the
most absorbent material printed. This will always result in excess
ink when printing high-quality, high-holdout substrates. Top-quality
flexographic printing requires that the anilox roll be selected based
on the characteristics of the substrate and the graphics being reproduced. Modern flexo presses permit quick change of anilox rolls
and thus routine production of top-quality printing.

   The prohibitive cost of anilox rolls is also a drawback of flexo. A
10-in. narrow-web anilox will cost approximately $700–1,800, where-
as a 50-in. roll might be $4,000–7,000. In the case of very large cor-
rugated presses, the cost of an anilox can be more than many pay
for their automobile, $8,000–20,000. This necessitates printers
deciding what they will tool up to produce and limiting the assortment of substrates to a manageable range.

   Inventories of plate cylinders, particularly for larger presses, can
be considered a constraint for flexo. While variable repeat is a defi-
nite advantage of both flexo and gravure, it is also expensive to
develop an inventory of cylinders to cover the wide variety of jobs

that customers demand. The development of high-quality, light-weight plate cylinder sleeves will reduce this issue for those getting into flexography from now on. These systems are not new in concept, but are now sufficiently developed to be considered as total solutions by many flexographers.

THE INDUSTRIES

The flexographic printing process is a tool used by many different industries. To understand its place, it helps to know a little about these industries and their products. Many of the industry segments use flexo alongside of other printing methods. For example, the paper bag industry uses gravure and flexo, often side-by-side in the same plants. The tag and label manufacturers use flexo, rotary letterpress, screen printing, and both offset and gravure to a lesser extent. These processes are often mixed on the same press. This is particularly true of flexo and screen. The corrugated industry uses flexo and occasionally offset for printing on combined board. It uses offset and occasionally gravure for labels that are attached to corrugated products. It uses flexo and occasionally some gravure and offset for preprinting the linerboard, which is combined on the corrugator to become the outer surface of the corrugated container or display.

Applications are specific to industry segments because of their substrates, their converting processes (which often are in-line with printing), their end use requirements, necessary production speeds, and their unique equipment (as in the case of publications or envelope presses). It is common for elements specific to a product to define major constraints on the printing "system." High-speed presses that lack any drying provisions certainly call for special inks and often plates and aniloxes to achieve their print demands. Their solutions would be of little or no use to others whose applications permit sophisticated drying or curing provisions, just to pick one element of the system.

The following is a partial list of industries where flexography is the major printing method. Beside the industry is a name of an association which serves that industry segment and can be looked to for information specific to that application.

Tags and labels	Tag and Label Manufacturers Institute (TLMI)
Multiwall and other paper bags	Paper Shipping Sack Manufacturers Association (PSSMA)
Plastic bags and laminates	Flexible Packaging Association (FPA)
Corrugated cartons and displays	Association of Independent Corrugated Converters (AICC)
	Technical Assoc. of Pulp and Paper Industry (TAPPI)
Folding cartons and setup boxes	Fiber Box Association (FBA)
Envelopes	Envelope Manufacturers Assoc. of America (EMAA)
Newspapers and publishers	Newspaper and Publications Flexo Users Group (N&PFUG)
Flexographers (all uses)	Flexographic Technical Assoc. (FTA)
Educators (all types of print)	International Graphic Arts Education Assoc. (IGAEA)

Flexo printing is the same regardless of the application; how-ever, the challenges of the application are often sufficient to warrant special educational offerings for that segment. For example, the EMAA membership has flexo printing systems in line with diecutting, folding, and gluing and their production speeds are very fast. Combine this with the fact that they print on absorbent paper and have no dryers in most cases, the print problems are very specific. This scenario warrants special education and training programs tailored to their membership. The same case is easily made for almost any industry segment. Since these industries have their own associations, it is reasonable for programs on flexo printing to be offered alongside of other programs on their specific converting and business issues. It is important to understand that these industries' first businesses are making boxes, bags, labels, and envelopes. Printing is just a necessary process that supports the primary activity.

The FTA, on the other hand, centers all activities on the flexo process, just as the Gravure Association of America does with gravure and the Screen Graphics Imaging Association with screen printing. FTA meetings also have breakout sessions for specific industry segments. Most common among these are publication, corrugated, envelopes, and folding cartons. They also segment by scale, offering separate sessions for narrow-web and wide-web applications. The FTA also runs frequent special programs on current issues to help their members stay up with any technical developments that may affect their businesses.

Even educators have the IGAEA, which has technical sessions on flexography along with all printing processes and phases of production. Anyone interested in staying current on the printing aspects of their industry should be a member and active in association work. It is knowledge that separates people as well as organizations. Many individuals develop their knowledge via association activities to the point that they are sought for their expertise by employers and even become independent entrepreneurs by selling their consulting skills. Such technology leaders, of course, are constantly reading. In addition to books on flexo, which are very limited, there are many journals and magazines that keep their readers up with developments. A partial list of such publications may prove helpful to you as you seek more information to build on your background gained from this book.

Boxboard Containers
Converting Magazine
Flexo Magazine
Package Printing & Converting
Packaging World
Paperboard Packaging
Paper, Film & Foil Converter

In summary, the industries that use flexographic printing are numerous. To find flexographers in your area you would look first to the industries that convert paper, paperboard, films, and laminates into products such as bags, boxes, labels, and any other packaging products. You will not find many flexographers in the yellow pages under "printer" since they generally specialize in other specific manufacturing processes. It is this situation that makes it difficult to determine just how much flexography there really is.

IS FLEXOGRAPHY COMPETITIVE?

All printing processes compete on the same list of criteria—cost, quality, and turnaround/speed of delivery or "service." Today quality is possible with all the processes. All printing methods permit direct imaging from digital information. The interface with electronic design and prepress production is no longer a source of differentiation. Plate production and manufacturing throughput, however, are determinants in speed of delivery. Flexographic platemaking ranks second in speed to lithography but still is typically faster than gravure. Cost of plate production is still a major issue and one of the greatest advantages of lithography over other methods. Given ideal workflow, gravure cylinders can be competitive with flexo in terms of throughput time. If the share of the total pie of the printing market continues to shift toward flexography there should be benefits that come with "scale." More competition will also lower the cost of plates. It is not at all likely that the flexo plate, as it is presently designed, will ever be as economical as the litho plate. Once on press, however, the benefits of variable repeat and in-line converting favor flexography over litho. When combined with its ability to print on a broad spectrum of substrates (not one of gravure's strengths) the competitive picture for flexo is quite positive.

3   FLEXOGRAPHY WORKFL

This chapter provides a brief yet technically sound overview of the common workflows for flexographic print production. There are many alternative approaches taken by flexo printers, particularly by specialists in niche markets. This variety of workflows is not unique to flexography, however. The digital changes of the past decade have created new options in the entire printing industry.

Before there is production there must be design. Before there is graphic design there is generally structural design. Design for flexo starts with analysis of the customer and product requirements. Whether it is a simple label or a complex box, bag, or carton, the printing and graphic design must fit and complement the design of the structure. Successful graphic design must provide for the capability of the converting processes. Boxes and cartons must be diecut, folded, and glued. The graphics that wrap around these containers must allow for the variation that occurs where the two pieces join and glue. The same is true of paper and film bags. Customers first require performance of labels, boxes, and bags. Manufacturers require graphics that sell, inform, and look great too.

Communication begins with common elements. These may be words, pictures, photographs, or illustrations. Projects headed for print reproduction have defined purposes. These may be to sell, provide direction, inform, or warn of potential harm. The graphic designer uses these elements, and a structure to create a product that will satisfy all the requirements of the job. And yes, there is usually a budget.

ːSIGN REQUIREMENTS

The designer must not only have the talent to conceptualize a winning solution, but must also have knowledge of the capabilities of the printing process. A great design makes the solution achievable as well as profitable. This calls for knowledge of press capability: how much *trap* (register overlap) does the press require? How many colors are available? And how close will the converting fit the graphics, or vice versa?

In addition to converting requirements, most products have other end-use specifications. The following are just a few common ones.

- Product positioning affects panel position and location of desired as well as required elements.
- *Rub resistance* is the demand that a label not be damaged by the constant rubbing of one package against another or against the inside of a corrugated shipping container while being transported.
- *Fade resistance* is the requirement that colors not change through a specified amount of time in the sun or other light. The designer must know whether the product will be subjected to long periods of exposure to light.
- *Product resistance* is often required. Alkaline resistance is essential for a label used on a soap box or bottle. It must not be degraded by exposure to the high alkaline contents of the container.
- *Slide angle* is the requirement that bags or boxes not slide when a pallet load is being moved up a conveyor or by fork lift. This is achieved by application of a slip-resistant varnish on the stacking surfaces.

Other constraints must be included on the list for designers to consider as they design for flexo production. There are also many legal requirements to be met. We all know of the lists of contents. Quantities must be shown in specific places and sizes, and warnings are commonly required. Since flexo is the dominant process in packaging and other product identification, product colors are commonly required. Examples might be Coke red, Kodak yellow, or Armour blue. Since many presses are limited to six colors and most jobs require metallics and one or two varnish plates, designers must plan to substitute a product color for one of the traditional process colors—cyan, magenta, and yellow. The bottom line for the flexo designer is that many requirements come before the graphic design can begin. These must be engineered into the design for the project to be successful.

DESIGNING FOR SUCCESS

Designing for success is a process that starts with the customer communicating a dream and a sales or customer support person listening and contributing ideas. Great designers welcome a team approach and capitalize on the knowledge they get from each team player. They build on the strengths of the system and steer away from any known limitations. They work with the other team members and glory in the execution of a smooth running project. When the customer and the team members are delighted, they enjoy more business. Designing for success is a real win-win approach for everyone involved. No one is able to do it alone. As you will see in Chapter 11, there are many different flexographic systems. It requires a team process.

If the operating flexo press is a system, then graphic designers can know ahead of time the specific capabilities of that system. Common sense suggests that excellent projects will result from developing the designs to take greatest advantage of the system's capability. Some designers say, "I design great jobs; it is the printer's responsibility to produce them." These are inexperienced individuals whose egos exceed their desire to engineer a real winner. A real winner is a project that delights the customer and allows all in the production chain to be professionally and financially successful. Designers of "winners" spend more time on challenging and creative projects and less on rationalization over what went wrong with recent efforts. The designer is the most important player in any project. Great designers, however, understand they are part of a team. Their experience has taught them that not all printers are created equal. They know about the system in the printing and converting plant. They engage the production team early in the project. When several printers will be producing the job, they know to expect more variability among the systems. When designing for more than one printing process, they respect the added challenges to be met. Excellent designers understand the concept of "designing for success."

When the customer and designer agree on a substrate, many design factors have been determined. If the surface is smooth and glossy then low-volume aniloxes will be used. This enables the designer to use relatively fine screens, 100 to 150 lpi or higher, depending on the plates and press. The designer is free to include relatively small pictures, since fine-line screens support the optical illusion of continuous tones quite well. Register, on the other hand, is dependent on mechanical integrity of the press. The smaller the image, the more critical the register tolerance. The printer should be able to show the designer printed evidence of the press capability. It is expected that narrow-web presses register well, since most of their work is small. CI presses register well, but images printed "down stream" from the CI drum have more latitude and the designer must consider this in planning.

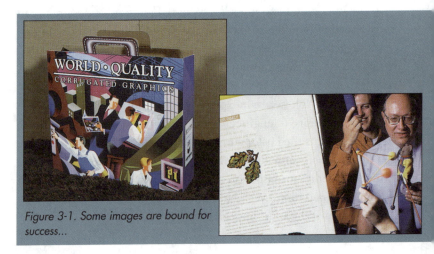

Figure 3-1. Some images are bound for success...

Images themselves can be specifications for success or for failure. For example, the hardest image to print by any process is a uniform tint. Trying to lay down a 30% flat tint over a large area is bound for trouble. We see the tiniest flaw in an even tint. Impression variation or any loss of ink film uniformity is a visible flaw. Dust, a single damaged dot, or a mark from a roller will cause a reject. In contrast, "busy" is easy to print. When there is a lot going on in a design, the viewer is entertained by looking around. The same slight flaws will not even be noticed. Such images are interesting and easily printed even with the common challenges that occur in print production.

The same descriptions as above are good to consider in selecting continuous-tone, black-and-white, or color originals. Photographs or artwork with large, flat, uniform areas invite disappointment. Photos with lots of detail, varieties of color and shades, and full range of tones from light to dark are bound for success. Photos with large subtle highlights and deep, subtle shadows are difficult at best. The designer and the entire production team will look bad, for certain, when these subtleties turn out virtually invisible in the printed product. No consumer cares enough about an image to study it. It either performs its purpose at a glance from the consumer viewing distance, or it doesn't work at all. Figure 3-1 provides examples of images bound for success and failure.

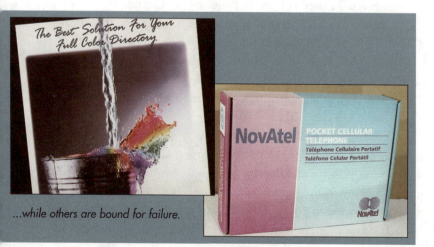

One more topic related to images and screens is *moiré*, objectionable patterns that come from superimposing two or more uniform and repeating patterns. Since the anilox roll has a uniform and repeating pattern of cells, it can be a contributor to moiré with the uniform halftone screen pattern in the pictures and screen tint areas. Today, with common use of high-line aniloxes this issue has become less common. In the case, however, where coarse rolls are used it becomes important to consider line count of screens in the graphics to avoid this problem. The moiré issue is also a concern with images containing uniform and repeating patterns such as shingles on roofs, chain link fences, and window blinds. As long as these are relatively large the problem is seldom experienced. If these images are very small they may result in *image moiré*.

Remember, the first of two hearts of the flexo process is the anilox roll. When the designer of a corrugated package or display knows that the aniloxes, which can't be changed, are a lower line count and higher volume than ideal for the high-quality liner that will be used, the elements of a successful design have been suggested. Bold, strong colors will be easy. Large solids will be no problem, but fine screens are out of the question. Using screens is not a problem as long as they are of a low enough line count to print clean. Well-printed, coarse screens look great and, assuming a large enough image, they will certainly not be as objectionable as would dirty print from screens that are too fine, in the same design. Reverses need to be designed with a more bold line weight to accommodate some fill-in from the high ink volume. Colors overprinting each other should be handled cautiously, since inks don't trap well over other colors that have not dried. Most corrugated presses do not have dryers.

"Know the limitations and design away from them," is always good advise. What flexo does best is strong and consistent color on the widest variety of substrates. What is a possible limitation is the reproduction of the lightest highlights. It is with reservation that this point is raised because many flexo printers do an outstanding job. It is common, however, to observe dirty print in the lightest highlights and objectionable voids where there was failure to hold the minimum dot either on the film or the plate itself. There is generally more dot gain in the highlights than with other processes and thus good design avoids excess challenges in these areas. Again, when the best practitioners undertake these images, they come away very successful. The role of the prepress members of the team is critical. Those prepress suppliers who specialize in flexo preparation know the demands and how to handle them. Traditional offset preparation will often come up short in dealing with demanding high-key images. (New technologies continue to reduce the highlight issues. Point-light plate exposure systems and laser imaging of the polymer plate are just two recent developments resulting in virtual elimination of the oversize minimum dot area.)

The use of gradations from solid to no dot at all is a challenge to all processes and possibly more for flexo due to its highlight gain. When a screen grades all the way to 0% the smallest highlight dot is usually at least 5–6% and often larger once its printed. The visual difference between no dot and a 5–12% dot is too much and appears as a dark line. Since we are in the business of delivering optical illusions, the correct way to achieve the objective of these graded screens is to carry a printable dot all the way to the lightest end of the scale. The viewer will see this as white and the customer will be happy.

Converting the printed design is another major factor that separates the excellent designers from their less prominent peers. Designers specify failure every day when they butt graphics against folds in cartons, bags, and boxes. There is always latitude in post-processing printed webs and sheets. Excellent designs account for the fact that the creases and cuts will move from a little to a consid-erable amount in relation to the graphics. Their designs allow this movement without appearing out of register on the product. Running fine lines across joints in a box or bag is a specified fail-ure. The same is true of building colors out of overprinted screens and bleeding them across the joining seams of a package. Any varia-tion at all causes a visual failure.

When there are great ideas that require critical register of images to structure, a meeting of all the parties to the project will generally find a way to achieve the dream. Latitude can be engineered into most jobs, although not without a cost. Remember every press is part of the reproduction system and some are capable of the utmost in tight fitting structure and graphics. Modern in-line and CI folding carton systems are in this class. Older presses are often limited in this same area, and these systems must have design allowances to assure their products appear as complete successes.

TRADITIONAL WORKFLOW

Whether done with the traditional artist's tools and materials or with the latest digital tools, the designer or design team develops a number of concepts from which to choose. These are simple images, commonly called "thumbnails," short for thumbnail sketches. Thumbnails are quick and very rough pictures of possible layouts. Thumbnails represent a visual brainstorming process. Customers decide on one or two concepts to be pursued further.

Figure 3-2. Desktop printer output of a job in progress.

These concepts are now developed into "rough layouts" to provide a more complete and realistic look at the design. From these "roughs" the choice is made of a design to be produced. Before full production it is common, but not required, to produce a "comprehensive" layout that is detailed, representative in color and size, and contains the actual sizes and styles of type. The comprehensive layout looks like the product. While this entire process may be completed with traditional artist's tools and materials (for example, colored markers and transfer type), today it is much more common for this work to be done using computers and software made for this purpose. Rough layouts and comprehensives are typically viewed from desktop printer output (Figure 3-2).

COLOR REPRODUCTION WORKFLOW

The clearest way to show the color reproduction workflow is by simple diagram (Figure 3-3). Most originals are in the form of a photograph. It is either a paper print, called a C-Print, or a transparency, also called a chrome, such as a 35-mm slide. Highest-quality originals are often large-format rather than 35-mm, since 35-mm requires excessive enlargement. Increasingly, digital cameras are used to capture the original subject rather than conventional photography. Digital cameras are actually CCD scanners linked to a camera and are capable of very good quality with subjects originating in studios.

Originals that are photographic or artist's creations—drawings and paintings—are scanned into digital files, using either a flatbed or drum scanner. The image is captured as digital information and imported into software for manipulation of tone, gray balance, color correction, and detail enhancement. It is assembled with the other text and graphics before being output. Digital camera images are imported to the workstation just as any other scan. The manipulations are often done in the original studio workstation when qualified people are at the controls. Rigid art and, sometimes, oversize artist's creations are still occasionally separated on a process cam-

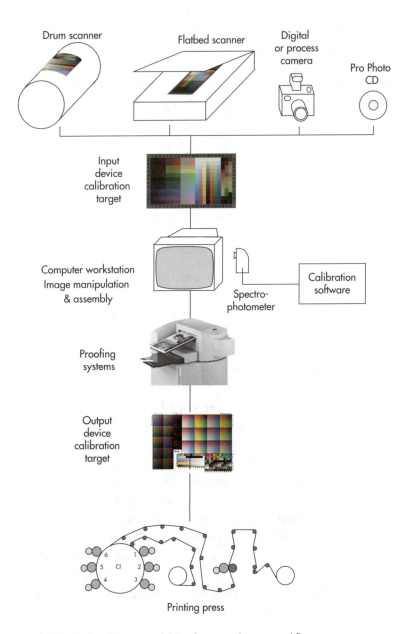

Figure 3-3. General concept of the color reproduction workflow.

era. This is very limited and will not be found without a search. Film is almost always proofed in one form or another to check accuracy of the output. When the customer needs to see a proof of final output, it is sometimes necessary to image a set of films with curves matched to the proofing system since plate films are cutback (compensated) for the printing system. Flexo printing is seldom a good match to most available proofing systems. Digital jobs may be checked using digital color proofs before output to film or plate. Digital proofs will, or have already, become the preferred method of predicting print results for flexo (but let the debate go on).

The issues of flexo color reproduction are generally the same for all printing processes, except for the uniqueness of the anilox inking system. Since the ink-film thickness may vary widely to accommodate the variety of substrates, it is imperative that prepress work be carefully tailored to the production components. Current developments in color measurement and color management promise to be significant in advancing the predictability and first-time successes of flexo projects.

TRADITIONAL PREPRESS AND FILM PRODUCTION

As technology changes, new tools and processes replace old. Such is the case in prepress production. At the time of this writing, traditional prepress methods and materials have declined to the point where one could debate its inclusion here. It is described here to help all understand how it has been done in the past and is still done in selected markets and locations where it continues to serve its purpose.

Starting with the layout as a plan to follow, the "mechanical artist" produces a pasteup. The pasteup contains marks to show where the graphics line up with the structure, folds in bags or boxes, and seams where two sides might glue together. The base art, the board itself, contains the dominant image, usually black. All the type is pasted in place, lines are inked, illustrations attached, and solid "windows" are positioned where black-and-white or full-color photography will be located. This is sometimes called the "base art" or "key" image.

There are many ways to prepare for additional colors and varnish image areas. In traditional preparation it is common to attach overlays for each color. The areas on the overlay may sometimes include type and line images as well as areas of color that fill in the illustrations on the base art. Think of these as the areas that a child fills with colors in a coloring book. The alignment of these colors with other images is called *register* and must be as accurate as possible. The edges of the fill colors must be cut to line up with the center of the lines on the base art. This provides the only allowance for misalignment as the printing press lays down each color over the others. The amount of overlap of registered images is called register trap (Figure 3-4).

Figure 3-4. In the top example, the cyan background is trapped into the magenta logo to avoid the white space that would appear if misregister occurred using knockouts (bottom). Both trap line and misregister are exaggerated here for illustration purposes.

The traditional *pasteup*, also called a *mechanical*, is next photographed on a process camera (Figure 3-5). (In a hybrid system, the mechanical may be scanned into a digital form for electronic imaging.) This converts each layer of the mechanical to a negative. The image areas are clear and the nonimage areas are opaque black.

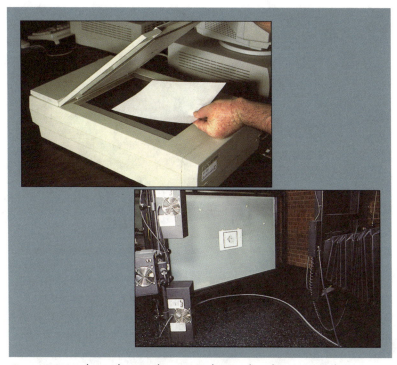

Figure 3-5. Mechanicals are either scanned using digital means, or photographed with a process camera to create negatives.

This negative is a light mask for imaging the next step in the production flow. The opaque/black areas must stop light from passing while the clear areas pass light freely. The negatives are inspected for density and flaws. The dimensions are carefully measured. Any pinholes, small clear spots caused by dust or a dirty pasteup, must be opaqued out. Opaquing is done by painting with red or black light-stopping material, covering all clear areas that are not wanted (Figure 3-6).

The negatives for flexographic platemaking must be shortened in the "around the cylinder" direction. When a relief plate—letterpress or flexography—is wrapped around a cylinder, it becomes longer in the wrap direction. This is called wrap distortion. The thicker the plate the more the distortion. The smaller the cylinder diameter the

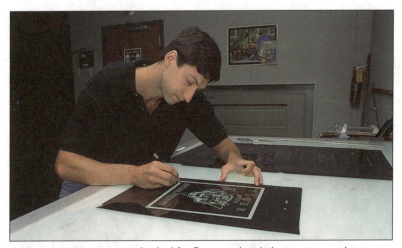

Figure 3-6. Negatives are checked for flaws, and pinholes are opaqued out.

more the plates elongate. Therefore there is no standard compensation for flexography. This is also why plates made for one printer may not be useable by another. Figure 3-7 shows how cylinder size and plate thickness affect the amount of distortion that must be prepared for in this step.

The original camera negative is contacted on a distortion device which exposes in a tiny line as the negative and duplicating film are passed under the light. By moving the negative slightly faster than the film being exposed, the new image is shortened. There are other methods used to achieve this one-direction distortion, including special cameras with "anamorphic lenses." Regardless of how this is accomplished, the flexo platemaker requires a negative to be the exact size, with the image right reading when the emulsion is up. For sheet polymer plates it is common to require a film with a highly matte emulsion to permit good drawdown against the plate surface.

ELECTRONIC PREPRESS AND FILM PRODUCTION

Today production workflow can vary considerably among printers depending upon the technology being used. Since there are too many hybrid approaches to attempt to detail, the classic scenario will be explained.

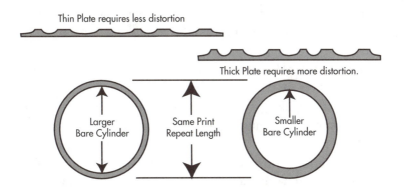

Below: To print the same image, there will be more elongation from a small cylinder. The cylinder on the left will elongate 15%. The one on the right prints only 7% longer.

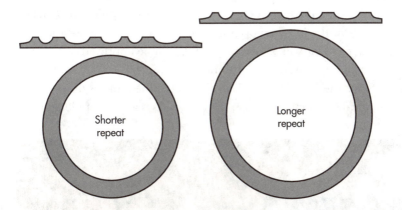

Figure 3-7. Plate cylinder size repeat length and plate thickness affect elongation.

As with traditional workflow, the digital designer creates the plan called a layout. The first stage still involves a visual brainstorming process that results in *thumbnail sketches*. This work may start as handwork but normally will be carried to completion using a desktop computer and one or more common design software applications. Many thumbnails are produced, from which a few are selected for further refinement. From these rough layouts the client, in conference with the designer and often others involved in marketing and production, selects the design for production. The designs may be evaluated on screen or from the output of a desktop printer or proofer.

At this point the designer may turn the project over to a production artist or **become** the production artist. Again, working on a desktop computer, the production artist creates finished art. This is a digital original containing all the type in the size, style, and color desired. Line illustrations such as pen-and-ink drawings are in place. All colors are shown exactly where they will be in the finished job. Pen-and-ink drawings are digitized into the desktop by a flatbed scanner. Photographs appear in size and position. They may be indicated *FPO*, which means "for position only." If so, this indicates that the actual original photographs will be supplied separately and digitized by the next player on this graphic reproduction team. Now the job is an original of exactly what the mass-produced product will look like. This work will again be approved by the customer or an agent of the customer (Figure 3-8).

Since the tools of the desktop are often the same as those of the technical production people, the next tasks may be completed by

Figure 3-8. Viewing a job on a monitor for approval.

the same or different team members. This operator must have complete knowledge of the production phases of the job. This is where the screen ruling or number of rows of dots per inch is determined. The type of screen must be entered—round or elliptical or even stochastic. Most jobs are run several images at one time. If there are four images on a plate, we say the job will be run "four-up." Jobs are run from one-up to many-up depending on the number required and the size capacity of the press and finishing equipment. The "one-up" production art must be multiplied by a procedure called "step-and-repeat." The number around the cylinder and the number across must be entered in the instructions. The amount of distortion (compensation for wrapping the plate around the cylinder) is determined by the size of the plate cylinder and the plate thickness. This must be determined and entered in the output instructions. Like all other printing processes, the flexo process prints with *dot gain* or image spread. This means that the images must be "cut back" or made to print less by a calculated amount on the plate. This way, after the image gains or grows (darkens) on press, it looks exactly like the design the customer approved.

Next the job is proofed on a digital printing device. A proof is a hard copy of the job and is used to check all details for accuracy. There are many proofs used as needed along the way, but there is always one at this stage, just before the job is committed to film. Film output is an expensive step if the job is not correct. Proofs may be very accurate and look just like the final printed product, or they may be quite crude. The difference is sophistication of the technology. The cost is proportional to the level of sophistication. If the proof looks crude compared to the product, it is not very expensive. If it is a very close likeness it is going to cost considerably more. Digital proofs may cost as little as a few dollars to several hundred dollars depending on the technology and size.

Once the proof is approved by the customer the job is output, normally to film that is used for platemaking. (If the plate is produced direct from the digital file, this would be done now.) The film is checked very carefully for size, especially the correct distortion, density (the light stopping quality), and accuracy of image. The final film is usually proofed on an overlay proofing system (Figure 3-9). The overlay has one layer for each color. It is handy to evaluate each color separately and also to see the amount of image overlap, called trap, to be sure the images will fit when run on press. The overlay proof is the most valuable in the pressroom to see exactly what is in the films. It is common for press operators to try to improve on a job when the problems are in the plates. When this happens they can do nothing to solve the problem. The overlay proof shows them such things and prevents much wasted time and expense.

Sometimes the job is output first without any compensation for flexo press gain. This is done to produce an analog proof. An analog proof is one made from film and is supposed to look like the finished job. This would be used for customer approval instead of the digital proof. Of course, this is an extra expense and is time consuming. It has been a common practice in the past due to the lack of a proof suitable for flexo. The digital proof is a better solution now that systems are available that can account for substrate and the many different production alternatives, including types of plates, sticky-back, and ink sets.

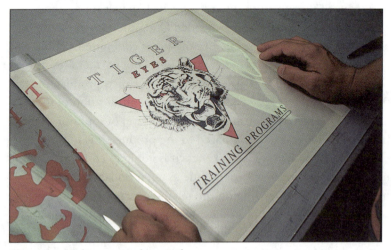

Figure 3-9. Making an overlay proof.

PLATEMAKING PRODUCTION FLOW

There are two generic types of flexo plates: rubber and photopolymer. Chapter 8 will detail both (Figure 3-10). First I will outline the rubber plate production process since it is the type of plate that dominated the industry for years and is still the workhorse in some markets.

A negative is used to expose a metal, or sometimes a hard photopolymer, pattern plate. The metal plate material has a light-sensitive coating that is also resistant to acid etchant. The exposed plate is developed and the now-unprotected metal surface is etched away. This leaves an image area which stands up above the etched non-image area. This is called a *pattern plate*. The pattern plate is used to make a *matrix*, which will be used as a mold to form the rubber printing plate. The pattern plate is placed face-down against a special matrix board and inserted into a heated molding press, also called a vulcanizer. The pattern is pressed into the matrix to a specified depth for enough time to form a perfect female (opposite) image of the pattern plate. After the pattern and matrix are removed and inspected, the matrix is placed back into the molding press and covered with a sheet of gum rubber. Under heat and pressure the press molds the rubber into the matrix to form a copy of that original pattern plate. The finished plate is carefully inspected for any flaws, the uniformity of thickness over its entire surface, and the depth of relief. It is now ready for mounting on the press.

Note that the rubber plate is the third generation of the image. It is also important to know that there is shrinkage in the rubber platemaking process. As the pattern plate is heated it expands, and as the matrix cools it contracts or shrinks. This action occurs again as the rubber is molded from the matrix and must be accounted for in the art and/or film preparation.

The photopolymer plate, as its name implies, is produced from a light-sensitive plastic material. Before the material is exposed it is unstable, easily molded, and useless as a plate. After exposure it is like rubber, durable and resilient. The negative for photopolymer

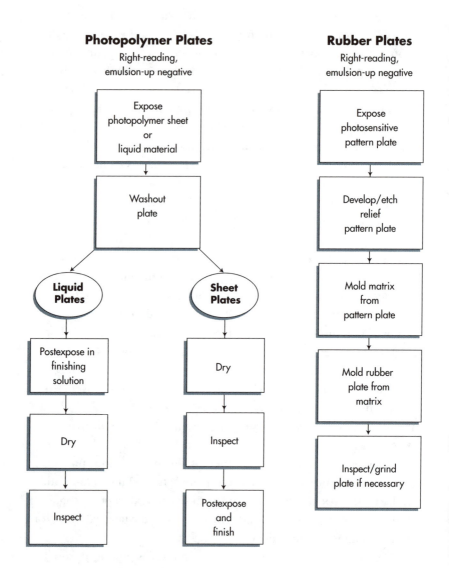

Figure 3-10. Platemaking production flow.

platemaking is different from that for rubber. It is only compensated for wrap distortion since there is no other size change in the process. Photopolymer plates start in either a precast sheet or a liquid form. The platemaking process is fundamentally the same although the equipment and its appearance are totally different. The plate is first given an exposure from its back or base (nonimage) side. This exposure is carefully timed to penetrate into the material far enough to form the floor of the nonimage area. Next the plate is exposed through the negative, which passes light only in the image areas. The light from the face exposure hardens the image areas while leaving the nonimage areas unchanged. The exposed plate is then processed in a solution that dissolves the unexposed material. It is literally dissolved and rinsed away, leaving the relief imaged plate. After checking quality the plate goes through a finishing process and is dried, ready for mounting on the press. Direct imaging from the computer to the plate is also accomplished in both rubber and photopolymer.

PLATE MOUNTING

There are two general approaches used to prepare plates for the press (Figure 3-11). In most webfed press applications plates are mounted directly to cylinders, which are then installed in the press. On corrugated and some other sheetfed presses the plates are mounted to a carrier sheet, which is outfitted with the necessary devices to attach it to a fixed plate cylinder in the press. The plates for publication presses are simply clamped directly to the plate cylinders with no "off-press" mounting required.

There are numerous methods used to accurately position the plates onto the print cylinders or carriers. Historically this has been one of the most skilled aspects of flexo production; however, the newest methods use sophisticated technologies to replace operator craft skills. The accuracy is equal to that of other printing processes. Unlike offset lithography and screen printing, there is no option for angling plates mounted directly to cylinders. Therefore, the register of the printed job can be no better than the mounting preci-

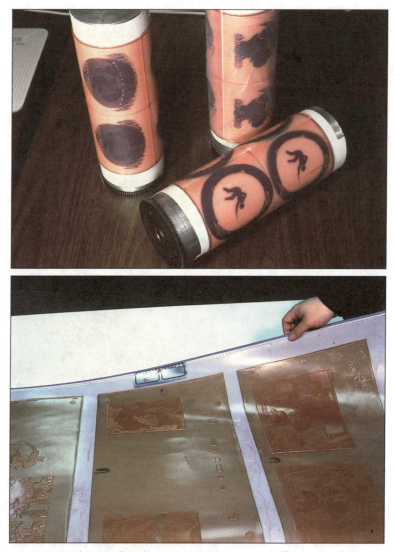

Figure 3-11. Flexographic plates can either be mounted off-press to cylinders (top) or left as sheets until mounted directly on press (bottom).

sion. Chapter 9 offers a more detailed explanation of the plate mounting processes.

PRESS AND FINISHING

Flexo presses are either webfed or sheetfed. Most are web presses and vary greatly in size from as small as 4–6 in. to as large as 100 or more inches wide. Sheetfed presses are used to print on corrugated board and may be as small as 7½×13½ in. to over 100×200 in. (Figure 3-12). Some envelope presses print sheets that have already been cut into the shape for converting into envelopes. There are a few other sheetfed applications that make up a relatively small portion of the total flexo production. With such a wide variety of sizes and applications, it becomes easier to understand why the flexographic industry is subdivided into so many industry segments. One basis for segmenting is by press types and sizes. These segments are narrow web, wide web, and corrugated.

Presses are generally classified by their designs; three are widely used. The in-line press is the most common in small press applications and is popular in the 24–32 in. press widths. The in-line press is simply a series of print stations connected one after the other in a straight line. Stack presses are designed with one print station above another, requiring less floor space but often requiring the operator to climb up to work on some of the units. The third style is the central impression (CI), also correctly called common impression design. This style has had significant influence on the growth of flexography, because it permits control of very lightweight and extensible (stretchable) films. The printing of films, foils, and laminants has been popular in recent years, as anyone who visits the supermarket will attest. The CI press holds the substrate in fixed position while it is printed in as many as ten colors. This is not to suggest that CI press applications are limited to these light and flimsy materials. They are used to print anything from the lightest to many of the heaviest substrates, including paperboard for liquid carriers, six and twelve packs, cases, and other folding cartons. More detailed discussion of presses is found in Chapter 10.

Flexo presses are also sometimes "converting" machines. They not only print but diecut, laminate, and sheet the freshly printed web

Figure 3-12. (Top) web unwind station and (bottom) sheet feeder.

into a finished product. The narrow-web segment of the industry expects presses to perform a multitude of in-line finishing operations, which is the reason that much work is moving from other processes to flexo. In-line converting is also common on larger presses, however the versatility is seldom as great. Larger presses are usually designed for specific market segments, such as folding cartons, multiwall bags, or shipping containers. Therefore the converting is unique to those markets. Many flexo presses do little or no converting, leaving such operations to off-line processes. Most printed films are fed from a roll and rewound onto a roll at the other end. Some do, however, slit the roll into multiple webs for rewinding.

Most web presses are equipped with dryers. Most corrugated presses are not. Many presses are capable of being registered while running, but others must be stopped to make changes in register. Many labor-saving devices may be installed on modern flexo presses to maximize productivity time while assuring no compromise in print quality.

OFF-LINE CONVERTING

While converting in-line is common, there are also many applications of standard off-line finishing. It is common to print multiwall bags from roll to roll and move the printed rolls to bag making production machines. This is also true of printed films that are laminated and converted to pouches and other styles of packaging for meats and vegetables as well as overwraps for numerous consumer items. The specifics are far too numerous to list.

4 REPRODUCING TONES AND COLORS

Tone and color reproduction are achieved in flexography just as in all other printing processes. The anilox inking system, however, does require customization of the prepress work to achieve optimum results. This chapter explains the principles of tone and process-color reproduction. It covers flexo-specific issues throughout to help those with prior experience in other printing methods realize where differences must be considered.

CUSTOMER DREAMS AND OPTICAL ILLUSIONS

Customers usually do not care about printing technicalities. They have dreams and purposes to be served by printed products. The appearance of the product is foremost. It is the goal of each player in the design-to-product team to achieve the customer's dream as closely as possible. We have a language to describe the elements of this image. Type and other solid ink areas are referred to as *line* images. Photographs are called *continuous tone,* often shortened to *CTs.* Continuous-tone images, including artists creations, are either black-and-white (monochromatic) or color. Most jobs contain both line and continuous-tone images and are referred to as *combinations*.

Printing presses are not able to vary the thickness of ink film to create tones within a single printing unit. Therefore, optical illusions called *halftones* are required. Halftones are made by converting tones to tiny dots, too small for the unaided eye to see. The viewer is fooled into seeing tones where none exist.

In flexography it is common to debate the best way to handle the *combination*, line-and-halftone, job. The anilox roll that is ideal for a large solid may carry more ink than the one considered best for halftones. Figure 4-1 provides a visual reference for a variety of line and tone images.

TALKING ABOUT TONES, DOTS, AND SPOTS—A VISUAL DICTIONARY

When discussing various tones from light to dark, the term often used is *density*. Density is a measurement calculated from reflectance, that portion of the light striking an area that is reflected back to the viewer. If a white area is measured, it would have a low density, perhaps 0.10. A printed black line image might have a density of 2.0 or higher. Tones are reproduced by translating the reflectance (density) into dot sizes.

Tone and color reproduction require knowledge of the language of dots. The size of the dots should be determined by the distance from which the reproduction will be viewed. The farther away the image, the harder it is to see the dots. Billboards may have as few as a dozen rows of dots per inch. This would be referred to as 12 lines per inch (lpi). A close-up view looks terrible, but from

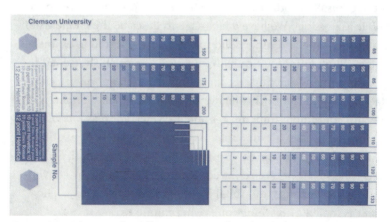

Figure 4-1. A basic anilox roll test image used to identify the optimum roll for a given production scenario.

100–500 feet the image appears to be a photograph. At the other extreme, pictures appearing in magazines normally need to have 133–175 lines per inch. The smaller the picture the closer the viewer tends to look at it. Therefore, small images need to have higher screen rulings or lpi.

Dot percent is the next element of the language of dots. Along with screen ruling, dot percent defines the size of a dot. A solid area is 100%. No dots at all would be 0%. A small dot, 5%, would appear very light and would represent a *highlight* area in the reproduction. A 50% dot covers half the small unit of space, leaving the other 50% white paper. This is considered a *midtone* and looks gray to the viewer. A 90% dot covers all but 10% of the paper, appearing nearly black. This is considered a *shadow* dot. Of course a tone scale is reproduced using the complete range of dot sizes and fools the human observer into seeing all shades of gray from white to black. The whiter and smoother the substrate the brighter the highlights in the reproduction. This same surface provides the blackest shadows since the ink remains on the surface. In reality the highlights come from the paper reflectance, and the shadows come from the ink absorbency. The difference in the density of the paper and the density of the printed shadows is the *range*. It pays to use good materials to achieve the best tone reproduction.

Before leaving *dot size*, it is important to mention the phenomenon called *dot gain*. While often discussed as if a disease of some sort, dot gain is really just part of printing. Very simply, as impression transfers the film of ink from the plate to the substrate, squeeze pushes some ink to the edges of the dot. As happens when you step on a drop of liquid, it grows, so does the size of the printed dot. It is only a problem when it is excessive or out of control. Routine print tests determine what change in dot area results at each step along the scale from highlight to shadow. These increases are compensated in the job prior to going to film or plate. This is commonly referred to as *cut back* or dot gain compensation, and is adjusted in a curve in the digital prepress process just before imagesetting. Figure 4-2 shows the curves for a typical flexo scenario.

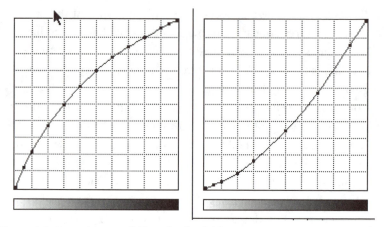

Figure 4-2. Dot gain curve (left) and cutback/dot gain compensation curve (right) typical for the flexographic process.

Screen angle is a very critical element in achieving the successful optical illusion. Any time a single-color halftone or any screen pattern is printed, the rows of dots should be aligned at 45°, the least visible angle; 90°, straight up and down, is the most visible. Screens should never be printed at 90° unless four or more screens are required in the same area. This is a very important principle for desktop publishers to follow. Figure 4-3 illustrates this principle clearly. As you look at Figure 4-3, move back until the dots become tone. Which screen angle becomes invisible first? We will return to this topic as process color is explained.

Spots are sometimes used in place of *dots*. Where dots are uniformly spaced in rows and vary in size to create the illusion of tones, spots are all the same size and vary in frequency (number used) to create the visual tones. This approach is known as *frequency modulated (FM)* or *stochastic* screening. Where very few spots are printed in a unit of space, the reproduction is light. Where a great many of the same size spots are packed into an equal unit of space, the result is dark or a shadow. Figure 4-3 shows the same image in conventional halftone screening and FM or stochastic screening.

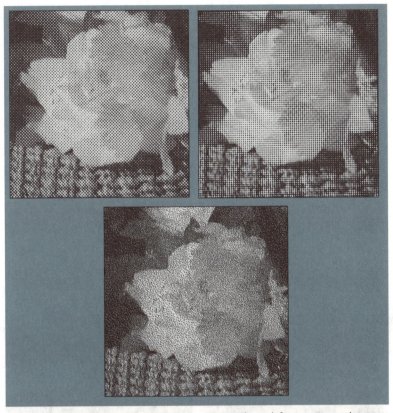

Figure 4-3. The same image showing conventional (top left) 45°, (top right) 90°, and (bottom) stochastic screens.

Why one screening approach over the other? There are two issues that relate specifically to flexo. First, achieving the lightest possible tones is a challenge. With conventional screening, the smallest dots are spaced equally with the larger sizes. This defines the lightest tone. In FM screening this same size dot, spaced farther apart, results in a lighter tone. The second clear benefit of FM screening is the freedom from *moiré*. Moiré is the objectionable pattern that sometimes results from two or more uniform patterns being superimposed over one-another. In order to print two or more conventional screens together, each must be angled 30° from the other. Figure 4-4 illustrates a moiré pattern resulting from two halftone images and a successful reproduction from angling the two 30° apart. In flexography it is possible to produce moiré with just one halftone image. This is caused by the uniform pattern in the halftone interfering with the uniform pattern of cells in the anilox roll. To avoid *anilox moiré* it is common for all flexo screens to be rotated 7.5°. FM screening removes the potential for moiré with the anilox roll.

Figure 4-4. Moiré patterns result from incorrect screen angles, as seen in the image on the right. The image on the left has correct screen angles 30° apart.

One must understand the reproduction of black-and-white CTs using halftones before attempting to learn how color is reproduced. This is because full color, normally referred to as *process color*, is also reproduced by printing halftones in three colors plus black. The combinations of dot sizes and ink colors result in a broad spectrum of colors. With conventional halftone screening each image must be screened at an angle of 30° from another. Figure 4-5 illustrates the multicolor dot pattern; the angles can be easily seen. Since three images use up all the 30° angles that are available, one halftone must be compromised. Yellow is the least vis-

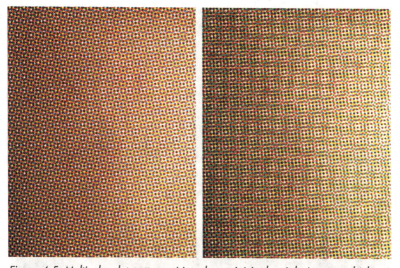

Figure 4-5. Multicolor dot patterns. Note the moiré in the right image, which results from switching cyan to the 90° angle normally used for yellow (which can't be seen).

ible ink. Therefore, yellow is angled halfway between two other images. It is customary to print yellow at 90°. (Why not use 30° or 60°? For flexo 60° would be bad since anilox cell angles are commonly at 60°.

HOW COLOR IS CREATED

The source of all color is light, the sun being the best of all. To demonstrate that sunlight actually contains all colors, Sir Isaac Newton used a prism to diffract the different wavelengths of light, which resulted in a *spectrum* of colors from red at one end to violet on the other. Newton also found that predominant bands of color within that spectrum (*red, green,* and *blue*) would add up to white. To test this, three lights, one of each color, are illuminated at the same time. The result is white light. You can demonstrate this to see for yourself. Figure 4-6 illustrates the separation of white light into the color spectrum, and Figure 4-7 shows the demonstration of color addition to produce white.

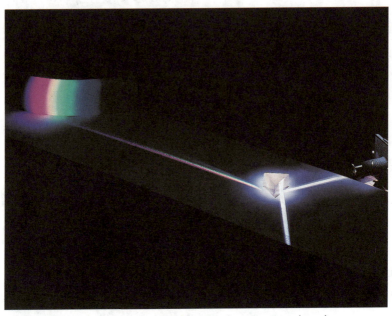

Figure 4-6. The separation of white light through a prism into the color spectrum.

Figure 4-7. Demonstration of the additive color principle.

Actually, there are two very common applications of this *additive color theory*. Most common is the color TV or your color computer monitor. It creates the full-color images that you see by the addition of exact amounts or intensities of red, green, and blue. Another convincing demonstration is found in theater lighting. It is common to find, if you look up into the light sources above the stage, the lighting is primarily a multitude of red, green, and blue spot lights. By varying their intensities the mood is delicately adjusted to complement the theatrical production. Additive color applications require three sources of color to create a spectrum of hues.

The three primary colors can be combined two at a time to create three secondary colors. Red light added to blue light results in a secondary color called magenta. *Magenta* could be called a blue-red. When blue and green lights are added together, the secondary color *cyan* is produced. Cyan contains full intensities of blue and green. The third secondary color is produced by turning on the red and green additive primaries, resulting in *yellow*. Therefore, yellow contains both red and green. Each of these secondary colors is missing or "minus" one primary. (Yellow is –blue; magenta is –green; cyan is –red.) Full intensities of all three lights result in white light. Of course, mixing the intensities of all three additive primaries will result in virtually any color you can imagine. These observations are important to understanding the reproduction of color with ink on paper.

Printed color images work exactly in reverse of the additive approach where lights are the source and are varied in intensity. In printing the color must come from the substrate and the light used to view it. Therefore, to reproduce full-color pictures the paper must reflect all portions of the spectrum. White is the only "color" that contains all colors. The light used to view the reproduction must also contain all colors—it must be white too. The printing inks are used to absorb or subtract some of the color. When the inks are printed over each other they must produce secondary colors. Many colors, when printed over each other, produce black. Black is the total absorption of light, thus it has no color.

The best colors for reproduction of the largest spectrum of printed color are the additive "secondaries." Cyan, magenta, and yellow are the printer's *subtractive primary colors.* Each of these colors contains two-thirds of the spectrum. Cyan reflects green and blue, magenta reflects red and blue, and yellow reflects both green and red. Each of these colors is missing one third.

To print process-color, yellow, magenta, and cyan ink separations are printed proportionally to their presence in the original. If cyan is printed first, it will print in high percentages where the original contained blue and green and not red. Cyan ink stops the reflection of the red light from the white substrate. Next, magenta is printed, absorbing the green reflecting from the substrate. Magenta, containing a full dose of red and blue, prints heavily in red and blue areas. Magenta is minus green so would not print where the original contained green grass and leaves. The reproduction now appears very blue since the green and red have been removed where they were not present in the original. Last, the yellow or "minus blue" is printed, absorbing blue everywhere it was missing in the original. Now the reproduction looks like the original. Where minus red and minus green are both printed, we see blue. Where minus green and minus blue are printed together the image appears red, and where minus blue and minus red are both printed, but without magenta (minus green), we see the color green. Of course, most colors are not pure red, blue, or green. By varying the halftone dot percentages of each process color, the spectrum of colors can be created. Figure 4-8 shows how the subtractive primaries act as filters to selectively absorb colors, resulting in the appearance of a full-color picture.

As explained above, ink colors are assumed to be perfect matches to the additive secondaries. Since colorants are pigments, the actual colors do not match the light-based theoretical model. This means that overprints of all three colors may not produce a true black. To achieve the greatest density, and thus range from paper-white to black, the printer also uses a black ink image. Hence, the reproduction of full color is referred to as *four-color*

Figure 4-8. Demonstration of the subtractive color principle.

process. This discrepancy between the theoretical and the actual CMY colors/hues causes other challenges.

OBJECTIVES OF COLOR REPRODUCTION

There are four generally accepted objectives to be achieved in all process-printing projects. They are (1) tone reproduction, (2) gray balance, (3) color correction, and (4) detail enhancement or sharpness control.

Tone reproduction is the rendition of tones from light to dark. A great reproduction shows the difference between two shades in a good original as visually the same two shades in the reproduction. When an original is flat looking, the tones in the reproduction can be adjusted to improve the final appearance. The goal is to enable the viewer to see all the levels from light to dark and the detail contained throughout the scale. In software with tone and color controls, these attributes are adjusted using curves. Figure 4-9 illustrates the two simple examples just described. Curves may be adjusted for

Figure 4-9. Curves are adjusted to improve tone reproduction (left) and color balance (right).

entire images, one color at a time, and even for selected portions of all or any color(s).

Gray balance has to do with reproducing shades of gray using cyan, magenta, and yellow, CMY. This is generally accepted as one of the top two criteria for a successful reproduction, right after tone reproduction. People know that certain objects are gray, black, or white. When such items reproduce with a color cast, they are immediately seen as flawed. Therefore, gray balance is a critical component of quality in color reproduction. In principle, gray would result from printing equal percentages of all three process colors. Each would absorb the same percent of red, green, and blue resulting in a balanced reduction of reflectance. Less light reflecting from a white area is a "gray" area.

Remember that all pigments are not matched in hue (color) to the light model. Because they are not perfect absorbers and transmitters of the colors they represent, adjustments are necessary in prepress. The term used to denote this difference between the actual pigments and their theoretical model is *hue error*. Hue error means that cyan ink, for example, which is supposed to reflect pure blue and green and no red, actually does neither. It absorbs a little blue and green and allows some red to be reflected. The same general issue is also true for magenta and (though considerably less) for yellow. Gray balance requires that the percentages of each process color be adjusted so the visual result is neutral, or gray. In general, neutral grays result from printing slightly more cyan than magenta and yellow. The specific amounts must be determined from press tests and may vary considerably among different sets of process inks. There are many different pigments used in process printing so this is not "standard." Because of the many end-use requirements across the spectrum of flexo applications, this is more an issue for flexographers than offset printers.

Color correction is the adjustment of the three process colors to achieve the desired outcomes in color areas of the reproduction. Color correction is inherently necessary because of hue error. Color is also commonly adjusted to achieve editorial desires. In other words, the customer wants a different color than what appeared in the original. Since many originals are really photographs of the actual original, the imperfections in the photographic medium must also be corrected. Whatever the reason, color correction is necessary to achieve the customer's dream. Color correction is listed third in priority because we, humans, really don't know

Figure 4-10. An image (top) shown with color correction (middle) and with unsharp masking (bottom).

whether a color is exactly right or not. People have very poor color memory. Color correction aims at improving the attributes of hue, lightness, and saturation (these will be further explained).

Detail enhancement or *sharpness* is considered the fourth major objective to be achieved as a color reproduction is readied for printing. The control of this attribute is referred to as *unsharp masking (USM)*. As with many terms, the origin of this terminology is in historical methods employed to adjust sharpness. USM allows the technician/artist to increase or decrease the visibility of detail. When the image is a model and the goal is to sell facial cream or powder, the visibility of pores or blemishes is undesirable. This calls for softening. If the goal is to sell bulky knit sweaters, and the texture of the weave is the enticement, there is generally a need to sharpen. The more USM, the more visible the detail. This process permits enhancing what is already in the image. It does not make sharp images out of those that are out of focus or add information not already present in the job. Figure 4-10 shows an image as it originated, then with color correction and finally with USM increased to show off the detail more.

COLOR AND ITS ATTRIBUTES

It is appropriate now to introduce just a little about color attributes and their measurement. Figure 4-11 is a diagram of the CIELAB, or L*a*b* color space. This is one of a number of systems for describing color. It is used to evaluate colors, specify target colors to be created or reproduced, and as one of the tools for adjusting colors during the reproduction process.

Roger Poteet, a great teacher and well-known expert on ink systems for corrugated packaging, explains the *L* or *lightness* attribute as an elevator running up the center of a round building. Since color originates in light, think of the center of the building as black-and-white. The elevator starts at the bottom, in the dark. As it rises to the top it gets lighter and lighter until it becomes pure white.

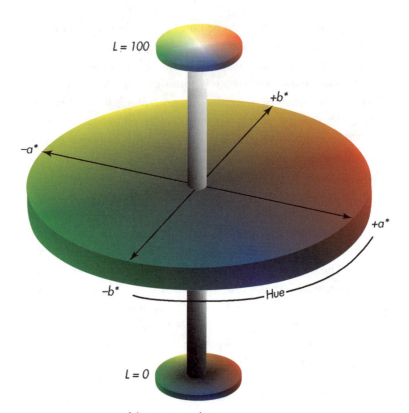

Figure 4-11. Diagram of the CIELAB color space.

As you go up in the "color space" building, the elevator stops, the door opens, and you exit. In the center of the building you are far from windows. It is very dim. Any colors seen here are rather dull. As you walk toward the windows, it becomes very light and the colors bright. Bright colors are said to be "saturated." As you examine the *a* axis of the L*a*b* diagram you see it is a scale from red to green. The colors near the *L* axis are very gray, not saturated. As you walk around the building you move from the *a* axis toward the *b* axis, the yellow–blue color scale. All the colors out near the edge of the space, by the windows, are brighter than those close to the *L* axis. If you reboard our elevator and rise to a higher floor, you exit to observe that you still walk around from red to yellow to green and finally blue. But all these colors or hues are now lighter. The building is really spherical in shape and at the top, so light that the colors are too light to discern from white. Any spot within this color space structure has an address or number. By identifying the position on each of the three axes, one can write the specific address or numerical value of any color. This information is basic to a number of other color specification systems.

Words are necessary to describe color, but are less precise than numbers. It is difficult to converse using numbers alone. Here are a few essential terms to help in your acquisition and communication of color knowledge. *Hue, saturation,* and *lightness* are the three dimensions used most commonly to define a color. First, *hue* is the color of an object, such as a red ball or green grass. Red is a hue. A specific hue of red would be best described with an L*a*b* (or other system) number. Any hue can be made lighter or darker. This is often referred to as the *lightness* or value of the color. A darker value of a specific color is a *shade* of that color. Shades are made by the addition of black when mixing colorants. With light, a shade comes from a reduction of the light. The shades are found on the bottom floors of our L*a*b* building. Lighter values are *tints* and are made by the addition of white. Go to the upper floors on the L*a*b* elevator for these. Printers often create tints by mixing the ink with the paper. They print dots, called tints, leaving paper between the dots for the human eye to blend. Intensity of a color is referred to as *saturation* or *chroma*. A brilliant, vibrant red is a very saturated color—it has lots of chroma. Go halfway up the L*a*b* building and walk to the outermost extremes to see these saturated colors. Only near the windows where there is good lighting will colors be bright and pure, or saturated. There are many other terms used by color scientists and technicians who specialize in color measurement and control activities.

COLOR PERCEPTION

Now that color theory and the objectives to be met by all involved in preparing color for print are clear, consider how the results might still be judged differently by various observers. While tools permit degrees of standardization, the use of a product by the ultimate consumer is anything but standard. Some see the package in bright daylight while others see it in fluorescent-lit stores, and still others in incandescent lighting. The different viewers are themselves nonstandard. Some are outright color blind while more are simply deficient in portions of the color spectrum. Some of the colorants used in printing inks are subject to change of appearance as they move from one lighting condition to another. While the color on the package matched the color of its contents in one place, it failed to match in another. This problem is referred to as *metamerism*.

For the reasons described above, certain color viewing conditions are recommended during color decision making. Proofs and printed sheets being checked for approval should be evaluated with control over lighting, environment surrounding the inspection surface, and ideally, but not always practically, the observer. It is common to require that all color decisions be made under standard lighting, 5000 Kelvin (5000K), in a special viewing booth with an ANSI-standard gray surface. The clothing worn by the evaluator must also be controlled so it does not reflect a color cast onto the product being approved. When the approval involves matching a product, it is imperative that the actual product, not a photograph, be compared side-by-side in the viewing booth.

There is no such thing as "color memory." The human observer is the weak link in this scenario. While there are tests to determine color blindness and deficiencies in color discrimination, they are not generally administered to qualify the customer or his agent to make such approvals. The best objective determiner of color match is instrument rather than human. A spectrophotometer standardizes the "observer" and is used routinely in other situations, such as the ink room. It is sufficient to say here that control, ideally standardization, of the lighting and the viewing conditions goes a long way toward making good decisions when evaluating color. The trend is toward far more extensive use of color measurement devices. The spectrophotometer is the tool for measuring color; its quantitative values are used in formulas to derive the numbers for any color specification system.

Color management suggests that all elements of the process be measured, calibrated, and controlled to achieve predictability and repeatability throughout the process. Pioneers in measurement and application are specifying by numbers, measuring all devices from monitors to proofers to presses to manage the process.

5 INK METERING SYSTEMS

F lexography can be distinguished from other printing processes by its inking systems. The metering roller is known as the
anilox roll, and it is the primary determiner of ink film thickness. It determines uniformity and consistency. Developments in
anilox rolls continue to be at the heart of process improvement. The
laser-engraved anilox permits use of doctor blades, which together
provide consistent image uniformity over long runs and over long
periods of time. All of this is essential for repeatability and predictability. Today flexography is competitive with all processes, largely
due to the modern anilox roll technology.

INK METERING

In every printing process there must be a method to meter the
quantity of ink. One must control the film thickness of ink in order
to use the least amount of ink required for density/darkness and
solid uniformity or coverage. Least is very important for two reasons. First, ink is a cost and least is best. Second, the more ink the
less control over growth of printing dots, necessary for the optical
illusion of *tone reproduction*. An important third issue has to do with
productivity. The less ink there is to dry, the faster this can be
achieved. Faster press speed equates to productivity and more is
obviously better.

Flexography borrows from gravure and the offset printing concepts to achieve its capability. I think of it as *pattern offset gravure**. A
gravure cylinder (anilox roll) prints a metered quantity of ink onto

---

* George Oswald

a resilient raised pattern, the plate image. The film of ink remains wet long enough to transfer ("offset") to the substrate which is impressed by the hard impression cylinder. As with gravure, if you desire a thicker film of ink, darker printing, you use cells that carry more ink.

The surface of the anilox roll is covered with tiny cells, all equally spaced and of the same depth and shape. The cells are specified by the number of cells to the linear inch and the depth of the cell, or its volume. They are often described as fine or coarse, depending on the cell count. A roll having 200 cells per inch is rather coarse, one with 400–500 cells per inch is average, and one having over 700–800 cells per inch is considered fine. Figure 5-1 shows that cell count alone does not reveal all one needs to know about the ink delivery capacity of the anilox roll. A 360-line anilox with a

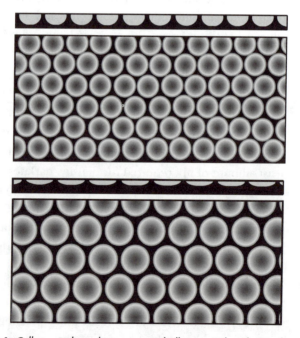

Figure 5-1. Cell count alone does not reveal all one needs to know about the ink delivery capacity of the anilox roll. A 360-line anilox roll with a deep cell (top) can carry more ink volume than a coarser 200-line roll (bottom) with very shallow cells.

deep cell can carry more ink volume than a coarser 200-line roll with very shallow cells. Therefore, when specifying an anilox one must always define the cells per inch or *cell count*, and either cell depth or *volume*. Cell dimensions are specified in microns. A micron is a millionth of a meter. To appreciate this, consider that there are 25.4 microns in 0.001 inch. Volume is measured in bcms, "billion cubic microns" per square inch (an interesting measurement combining a mixture of metric and English units). A volume of 1.0–2.0 bcm is a low volume, probably used for fine screens/halftones on smooth substrates. A volume of 4.0 bcm is a middle-of-the-road anilox roller while a 7.0 bcm roll is found where bold solids are being printed on a very rough and absorbent surface. To increase or decrease the amount of ink in flexography, one changes to another anilox roll that carries the desired amount.

The anilox roll is at the heart of the flexo process. There are several common forms of ink metering systems found on flexographic presses. The old standard system is called the "two-roll system" (Figure 5-2 top). The anilox receives a flood of ink from the fountain roll which is suspended in a pan of liquid ink. The fountain roll is run in tight contact against the anilox roll. The fountain roll turns slower than the anilox, creating a wiping action. This causes most of the surface ink to fall back into the fountain, leaving only the ink inside the cells on the anilox roll. The ink in the cells is then transferred to the plate as they come in contact. In the two-roll system, the efficiency of the wiping action is affected by the durometer of the rubber fountain roll. A harder, higher durometer like 80 wipes the surface (lands) of the anilox more efficiently than a soft roll with a durometer of 50. (The lands are the tops of the walls between cells which support the rubber roll or doctor blade and define the cells.)

The second metering system is a modified two-roll with a doctor blade. The rubber fountain roll is backed away so it floods the anilox with ink. The doctor blade is set at a reverse angle to the direction of rotation of the anilox. This *reverse-angle doctor blade* is engaged with

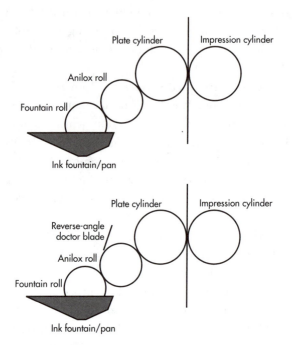

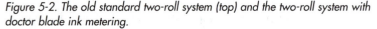

Figure 5-2. The old standard two-roll system (top) and the two-roll system with doctor blade ink metering.

just enough pressure to wipe the surface areas clean of all ink. This produces a much cleaner wipe than the two-roll system. Figure 5-2 bottom illustrates the two-roll with doctor blade ink metering system.

A third configuration of the metering system is the simple doctor blade design (see Figure 5-3 top) where the anilox is suspended directly in the ink fountain and the reverse angle doctor blade shears off the excess ink letting it fall back into the pan.

A drawback of all these designs is the open pan and exposed anilox. This permits free evaporation of the volatiles into the pressroom environment and the resulting change in ink viscosity (thickness) which affects printability. Pan covers are often used on large presses to reduce this effect and to keep out dust and other foreign airborne particles that contaminate the ink. Because of the in-line converting operations going on during the pressrun, dust is an important element to be controlled.

The last common print station design is the chambered doctor blade system. As shown in Figure 5-3 bottom, the pan is replaced with an assembly mounted against the anilox roll. On one side of the chamber there is a reverse-angle doctor blade that performs the metering function. The other side of the chamber is sealed by a containment blade, which keeps the ink from escaping or leaking out of the chamber. The ends of the chamber are sealed with gasket-like materials. Ink is pumped into the chamber and usually returned by gravity to the ink sump. The chamber blade metering system keeps the ink enclosed at all times, reducing the loss of volatiles and maintaining the ink in a constant and clean condition.

Flexography is a process where a precisely engraved anilox roll prints a thin film of ink onto the raised surface of the plate, which offsets the ink onto the substrate. It is imperative that the same amount of ink is delivered hour after hour and job after job if the

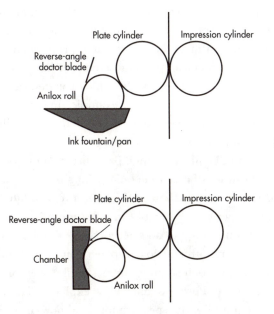

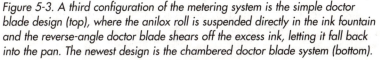

Figure 5-3. A third configuration of the metering system is the simple doctor blade design (top), where the anilox roll is suspended directly in the ink fountain and the reverse-angle doctor blade shears off the excess ink, letting it fall back into the pan. The newest design is the chambered doctor blade system (bottom).

process is to be predictable and profitable. Although there are many two-roll (sometimes called roll-to-roll) metering systems, the doctor blade is clearly the choice for repeatability. For some who prefer "art" over science, the two-roll system does allow the operator to vary the ink film. Of course, achieving the same variation on repeat orders poses a problem, complicated further when a different operator is at the controls. The best of flexo printing requires precise doctor blade metering, and the chamber blade system is the system of choice, at least until something better is developed. The flexo press is easily retrofitted with the latest metering systems; many older machines still in sound mechanical condition are being retrofitted to bring them up to the print quality capacity of much newer presses.

THE ANILOX ROLL

The anilox roll is a uniformly imaged gravure cylinder. Figure 5-4 illustrates cells of two specifications, showing the depth and the opening. It also shows the land area critical to print quality, including solid uniformity and clean printing screens or halftones.

The specifications of the cells in the anilox roll determine its capability for specific applications. For example, an anilox roll with 200 cells per inch, having a cell depth of 30–35 microns, will carry a volume of 7.5 bcm (billion cubic microns per square inch). This is a lot of ink. It would be like a six-inch paint brush, only good for very heavy applications of ink. You could paint a barn or rough siding with a six-inch brush and you could cover a very rough, absorbent kraft paper with a 200-lpi (lines per inch) 7.5-bcm anilox roll. However, if you wanted to do fine work, like fine lines and 133-line halftones on a smooth and coated paper you might want a 600-lpi 1.6-bcm anilox roll. Determining the best anilox roll for a given production scenario is a process that will be explained later; first an explanation is required of the specifications and how they relate to the substrates to be printed and the variety of graphics required to be reproduced.

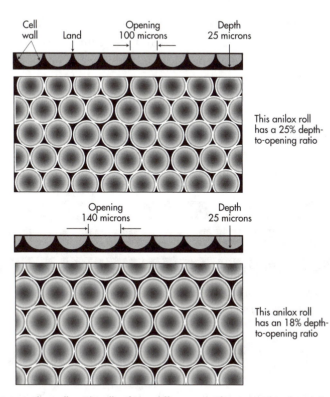

Figure 5-4. Anilox rolls with cells of two different specifications. This shows the depth and the opening, and the land area, which is critical to print quality, including both solid uniformity and clean-printing screens and halftones.

ANILOX ROLL SPECIFICATIONS

Cell count refers to the number of rows of cells per linear inch (specified to linear centimeters in the metric world—divide by 2.54 to convert). A cell count of 180 would be very coarse, found only in coating or low-end imaging applications where substrates are poor and quality is not a priority. A cell count of 360, once considered fine, is now a middle-of-the-road roll used in good work on absorbent paper and paperboard substrates. Today cell counts of 700 and above are commonly used for very high-quality imaging on smooth, high-holdout (not absorbent) substrates. This explanation places

importance on the substrate in choosing an anilox roll. Images, however, are also very important in determining the cell count.

Cell depth is the next specification and is just as important as cell
count. These two specs determine cell *volume*, which is the determiner of density in a given application. Figure 5-5 shows that three
aniloxes of the same cell count may have very different volumes
depending on the cell depth. It is volume that interests the printer.
When specifying an anilox roll determine the cell count and volume to do the job and leave the depth to the anilox supplier.

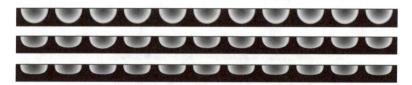

Figure 5-5. Three anilox rolls of the same cell count may have very different
volumes, depending on cell depth. The top roll shown here would have a 5-bcm
volume, the bottom has a 2.5-bcm volume.

Cell volume is the key to coverage and uniformity of solids.
More volume results in more ink and, thus, better coverage.
However, too much volume of ink also results in dirty print. If there
is too much ink to sit on top of the relief image of the plate, it will
flow over the shoulders and result in dirty print.

High-resolution images require high-line, low-volume anilox
rolls. There are rules of thumb for determining anilox cell count
from halftone lines per inch. It is common to demand at least 3½ to
4½ times more cells on the anilox than the lines per inch in the
halftone. This is to prevent *anilox moiré*, an objectionable pattern
caused by the screen of the graphics interacting with the anilox
screen pattern. Figure 5-6 shows the importance of the cell count to
the ability to produce clean printing. It can be seen that a high-line-
count ("line count" and "cell count" are terms used interchangeably) roll has enough cell walls to support very fine screened
images. A coarse cell will allow small percentage dots to fall inside a
cell, without being supported by a cell wall, and thus permit ink to

flow around the image onto the shoulder of the dot. This causes "dirty print" or dots to join wherever a dot is unsupported by a land area. A high-line-count fine anilox roll will produce clean printing of fine screens and type.

The best anilox roll specifications yield just enough ink to deliver the required density and solid uniformity while not overinking

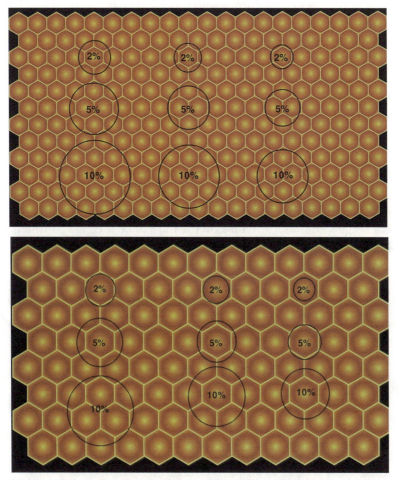

Figure 5-6. The importance of cell count to the ability to print cleanly.
The top shows a 900-line anilox roll with a 25-micron call opening and 3-micron cell wall; the bottom shows a 550-line anilox roll with a 42-micron cell opening and 4-micron cell wall. Images courtesy Harper Corporation of America.

the fine screens in the plate. This roll has enough cells to provide lands to support the finest image areas.

Cell angle can also be controlled. While traditionally the cells are angled 45° from the axis of the roll, it is possible to fit more cells into an area when they are aligned at 60°. Since this provides more cell openings and less land area, or space between cells, 60° rolls achieve better uniformity with less ink. The 60° angle is also better in avoiding moiré with traditional graphic screen angles since it no longer falls in line with the most desirable image angle of 45°. Today most new rolls are purchased with 60° cell angle.

Sometimes a flexo printer concludes that the ideal roll is a very-high-line-count, even when printing on an absorbent substrate. Then all that is needed is very deep cells to achieve the required volume. This introduces one last concept to be considered, *depth-to-opening ratio*. Figure 5-7 illustrates several depth-to-opening ratios. It shows that very high volumes might be engraved into an anilox of a high cell count. However, the bottom row illustrates that when the depth exceeds a certain point, no more ink is released to the plate. There is a range within which volume on the roll can be used to control ink film on the printed substrate. Beyond that range, no additional ink can leave the roll and there will be no increase in density.

Figure 5-7. Illustration of several different depth-to-opening ratios. Very high volumes can be engraved into anilox rolls. However, the bottom row illustrates that when depth exceeds a certain point, no more ink is released to the plate. Higher volume results in higher ink transfer, up to about 35% depth-to-opening ratio.

Until now the discussion might suggest that the anilox is the sole determiner of ink film thickness. But this is far from the case. The ink itself is a major player. It has been assumed that the amount of liquid that is printed controls the dry ink on the product. Actually it is the amount of solids, particularly the colorant, or pigment. Figure 5-8 illustrates that one ink may require 40% more liquid be printed to result in the same density and solid uniformity. This, of course, would require a 40% higher volume anilox roll. Such an anilox would not print as clean. Therefore, when people talk of high-line-count, low-volume aniloxes, you must realize they are also talking about inks with the maximum amount of pigment and the least amount of liquid necessary for transfer and adhesion.

Figure 5-8. One ink may require 40% more liquid be printed to result in the same density and solid uniformity. This, of course, would require a 40% higher-volume anilox roll, and would not print cleanly. In the illustration, the top anilox prints excellent density using a highly pigmented ink. The bottom anilox requires 40% more volume to print the same density because the ink contains less pigment and more liquid.

CHOOSING THE ANILOX ROLL

There are always several, if not many, considerations to be made in the choice of anilox rolls.

1. **Substrate.** If only one substrate is to be printed then the choice is easy. Many times one anilox roll must be used for a range of substrates. This calls for the anilox which delivers the least ink required to achieve density and solid uniformity on the most absorbent of these substrates.

2. **Anilox cost.** If one roll costs $15,000–20,000 for a five-color press, one may have to settle on just one or two sets of rolls for all one's needs. This is especially true in the corrugated industry. Therefore, even to print a variety of substrates and types of graphics, a compromise must be found for economic reasons.

3. **Time.** Modern flexo presses generally provide for quick changes of anilox rolls; however, most presses in use today are not so equipped. This means that to optimize the anilox to the job at hand, the changeover times may be prohibitive. Again, a compromise is necessary.

4. **Graphics.** It is common for customers or designers to specify graphics with fine screens on substrates of less than ideal surface. Since most jobs mix screens with solids this scenario presents problems. In this case the anilox will probably be chosen to achieve adequate solid density and uniformity while delivering more ink than necessary to the screens; another common compromise.

5. **Productivity.** While there are many influences on productivity, one common example is the availability or lack of dryers. The classic case is in the envelope world where very high speeds are expected without availability of dryers. Drying relies more on absorbence into the paper. The substrate is also generally rougher than ideal so that viscosities (fluidity of ink) must be lower, more liquid, and thus anilox volumes higher in order to deposit sufficient pigment for density and uniformity. Bottom line: fine screens are likely to suffer.

These realities point to the value of planning all jobs with input from the entire production team. It is unrealistic to expect a customer and designer to understand so much. Since everyone seeks a total success in any project, working together from the beginning will result in the best achievable results given the specific realities at hand. Chapter 11 discusses given printing scenarios in the context of a "system," which is essential understanding for optimization of production.

TYPES OF ROLLS

Laser-engraved ceramic anilox rolls are the dominant type of roll being used today. This is a steel roll that has been machined to very precise dimensions and tolerances. It has a plasma sprayed chromium oxide surface built up to a thickness of 0.006–0.010 in. The cells are burned into the ceramic with a CO_2 laser that literally vaporizes the coating, leaving a precise cell. The cell count and depth are computer-controlled, meaning that theoretically any specification can be set. This is one explanation for the rapid progress in anilox technology compared to the days when hard tooling was required to engrave the cells.

The ceramic surface is extremely hard, which is very important to print quality. Since high-quality flexo printing is achieved with doctor-bladed ink metering systems, the rolls must not wear or repeatability would be impossible. While ceramic rolls do wear, it occurs over an extended period of production.

CONVENTIONAL ENGRAVED CHROME ANILOX ROLLS

While today the vast majority of new rolls being purchased are laser-engraved ceramic, there are still many rolls in the industry of the engraved chrome technology. These rolls, also called *mechanically engraved*, or simply "chrome," are manufactured by a displacement process, the same as knurling. A hard, precise tool called a mill contains a male pattern of the cells (Figure 5-9). The mill is forced under tremendous pressure into the steel- or copper-covered steel roll. During several passes over the roll the cells are made deeper and deeper until the roll has reached full engraved depth. Just as ice dropped into a glass of water raises the level of water in the glass, this process displaces the metal up into the mill while the mill is pressing deeper into the surface. Since every cell is produced from the same "master" the conventional engraved chrome roll is a very uniform "gravure cylinder." The roll is electroplated with a hard chrome to provide protection from wear, hence the name engraved chrome. Figure 5-10 illustrates the two most common cell shapes used in flexo printing, quad and pyramid.

Engraved chrome has limitations that helped to move the market to laser-engraved ceramic, the greatest being its lack of resistance to the wear caused by doctor blades. Since new cell specifications require a lengthy process, demanding very high craft skills, to

Figure 5-9. A mill can be used to make the cells in an anilox roll.

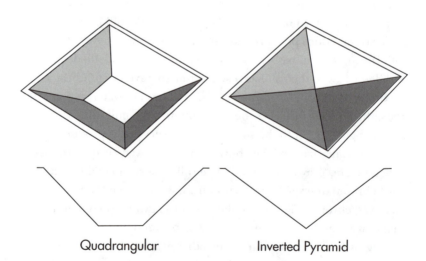

Quadrangular   Inverted Pyramid

Figure 5-10. The two most common cell shapes used in flexo printing, the quad and pyramid.

make the engraving tool, it was not possible to perform quality improvement experiments in a timely and economical fashion. These two factors were major contributors to the early acceptance of laser engraving as an alternative approach to anilox roll production. In little over a decade the dominant roll of choice changed from engraved chrome to laser-engraved ceramic.

There are other types of anilox rolls. Conventionally engraved rolls can be plasma-sprayed with ceramic instead of chrome and yield better life. These rolls are called *engraved ceramic*. This approach, however, has never been widely adopted. Another approach to anilox cell production is electromechanical engraving (Figure 5-11). This method uses the same machines employed in the production of gravure cylinders. The Ohio Engraver and the Helioklischograph are the two most common tools to employ a diamond stylus in cutting precise cells into a copper surface. The copper is then electroplated for wear resistance.

One last technique known as *random ceramic* has been employed. This is a roll which is simply plasma-sprayed with chromium oxide particles. The coarser the particle the more ink carrying capacity.

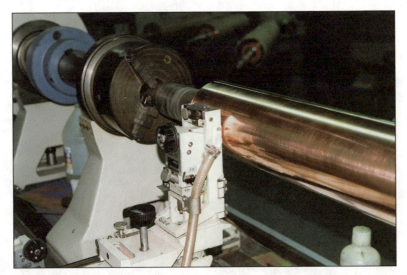

Figure 5-11. Electromechanical engraving.

Like sandpaper, the rougher the surface, the more ink, and the finer the particles, the less ink. This is a simple system, not as uniform in its ink delivery, and is used relatively little compared to other types.

Developments

Lightweight cylinders are now being used to replace the standard steel construction. Modern materials such as carbon fiber can be used to build the base roll without the weight of steel. These are much easier to handle, and shipping issues are reduced. At the time of this writing, these approaches were too new to offer conclusions as to their ultimate acceptance. The same is true of the use of sleeves, similar to those being used for plate cylinders. It is important to note that many new ideas continue to develop in this and other aspects of flexo printing, which is a sign of the atmosphere of change and development that characterizes flexo technology.

6 INKS FOR FLEXOGRAPHY

F lexo inks are fluid in form and are used primarily for the purpose of achieving color and density. Inks get color from pigments, adhesion from varnishes, and fluidity from the liquid or solvent. Inks must be printable and achieve end-use requirements in addition to the obvious appearance qualities expected by consumers.

The purpose for printing by any process is the mass production of consistent color and density on the customer's chosen substrate. Printing presses are electromechanical devices that bring together all the components at the right moment to complete the reproduction process. When printing problems occur, most of the people involved quickly point to the ink as the cause. My friend Larry Evans says of this phenomenon, "It's because there's never a problem until we put ink on the press."

I suggest it is because most printers know so little about ink. The factors that cause it to perform are chemical as much as physical and therefore are not easily seen. This chapter explains what ink is in lay terms. It details the multitude of demands, beyond color and density, that inks must achieve. Many who come to flexography from a commercial offset background find the end-use requirements of many flexo applications mind boggling. These requirements are generally far more problematic than the simple visual demands associated with achieving color and density. Remember too that flexo presses have no standard anilox roll. Therefore, color and density must also be considered differently from offset where the press operator determines ink film thickness and thus density.

TYPES OF FLEXOGRAPHIC INK

There are three common types of flexographic printing inks: solvent-based, water-based, and ultraviolet (UV) curing. Until the 1980s solvent-based inks dominated the process. In the 1980s water-based inks underwent major development, progressing from flat in appearance and difficult to print to the preferred system for most paper and paperboard applications. The driving force for this change was primarily environmental—the reduction of volatile organic compounds (VOCs) so harmful to the air and thus all living organisms. The most recent growth has been in UV-curable inks, driven by the same motivation, to provide a solvent-free solution for printing on films, laminates, and foils that have been very difficult to print with water-based systems. Outstanding quality is achievable by all three ink systems. In addition to color and density, quality attributes include solid uniformity, resolution or screen line count, and clean-print or freedom from voids, spots, and bridging in screens and clean edges on type and line images.

INK COMPOSITION

Ink is made up of three primary components: *pigment* or color, *resin*, and liquid or *solvent*. A fourth component is *additives*, which include a variety of components for enhancing performance. Ink is desirable for its color, but colorants are pigments and are of no working value by themselves. To be of use resin is added, which serves as the glue or binder attaching the pigment to the substrate. Like pigments, resins are solid and thus are not printable by themselves. To complete a basic ink there must be a liquid. In the case of solvent-based inks this is commonly a blend of alcohols. Water-based inks use water and amine for the liquid. Water-based inks are really pH soluble and water makes up the bulk of the "liquid." Ammonia is a simple amine and is sometimes used in these inks. There are more stable amines used in inks to keep them from changing quickly in the fountain of the flexo press. Inks also contain a variety of other components grouped under the title "additives." Additives include driers, waxes, surfactants, and other ingredients to enhance printability and end-use performance. The following table lists the relative amounts of the basic ink components in water- and solvent-based systems.

Component	Water-Based	Solvent-Based
Pigment	10–20%	7–22%
Resin	20–25%	12–30%
Solvent	50–60%	65–75%
Additives (incl. waxes)	1–6%	2–4%
Other amines	1–5%	

PIGMENT

Pigment provides the color. It is what customers want and is the most expensive part of most ink. Pigments are much like rocks in their original form and must be ground into tiny particles to be of use in inks. *Grind*, or particle size, has a major impact on print quality. Very coarse pigments prohibit high gloss, even though resin is the primary determiner of gloss. Rough surfaces aren't shiny. Fine grind is required for good density unless a very thick ink film is printed. Think of grind as a comparison between sand and rocks. A handful of sand will easily hide a white surface, while a handful of rocks would hide very little. The thicker the ink film the lower the quality. Pigment determines color fastness, resistance to fade. In multicolor printing, pigment combinations determine the achievable color gamut or range of colors. Pigment makes up anywhere from 7–22% of the ink volume. Pigment can't be used alone; it is a dry powder and floats uncontrollably in the air.

RESIN

Resin is the glue that attaches pigment to the substrate. Every particle of pigment must be totally encapsulated in resin. Resin is also the determiner of gloss. Resins for printing inks are similar to those used in paints and on floor coverings. Some are brittle and others are soft and pliable. Inks often use blends of resins to achieve required hardness, while not being so hard that they crack when folded or mark when contacted by another surface. Resins, which compose approximately 12–30% of the ink, are either natural or synthetic. Maleic resin comes from the pitch of pine trees. Acrylic resins are manmade. These are two common resins used in water-based inks. Like pigments, by themselves resins are hard and virtually useless.

Solvents

In order to make ink out of these two hard components there must be a liquid or solvent. In solvent-based inks alcohol is the primary liquid that dissolves the resin and produces the liquid ink. Solvent-based inks are *solutions*. Water-based inks are generally *emulsions*. Resins used in most water-based inks are emulsified in high pH. A mixture of ammonia or other amine and water is used to emulsify the resin and pigment and form the fluid ink. The liquid or solvent is also the determiner of drying rate or speed. Ethyl acetate is used to speed the drying of solvent inks. While not desirable, alcohol is sometimes added to water-based inks to speed drying. Propylene glycol is used to slow drying of both solvent- and water-based inks. Inks should be formulated by the manufacturer to dry as closely as possible to the ideal rate so pressrooms don't become ink laboratories.

The liquid or solvent is also used to control *viscosity,* the degree of fluidity of an ink. A high viscosity might be compared to cream, while a low viscosity would be more like skim milk. Viscosity is best measured using a rotational viscometer; it measures the resistance to stirring or mixing in units of centipoise. While not very accurate, press operators use efflux cups which are very easy to use requiring only a cup and a stop watch. Figure 6-1 shows two common efflux cups, a Zahn cup and a DIN cup. The efflux cup is a small metal cup of precise volume with a hole in the bottom of a specific size. Viscosity is measured as the time, in seconds, that it takes for the cup full of ink to run out through the hole in a steady stream. When the stream turns to a drip, the watch is stopped and the time is recorded. There are several efflux cups used by flexographers. The most commonly used, and least accurate, is the Zahn cup. Other efflux cups include the DIN, Ford, and Shell cups. The cups are numbered according to the size of the hole in the bottom. A no. 3 cup has a larger hole than a "2" cup and is used for more viscous, thicker, fluids. A typical viscosity reading might be "30 seconds, no. 3 Zahn." There is no single best viscosity for flexo inks. It is important to be able to measure and keep records to be able to

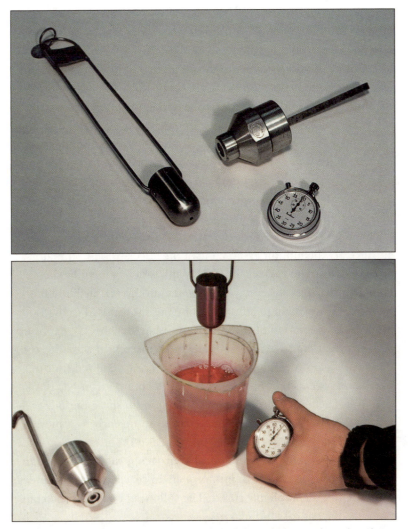

Figure 6-1. Two efflux cups (top), Zahn (on the left) and DIN (on the right). The bottom photo shows measuring viscosity with a Zahn cup.

repeat any process. Measuring and recording viscosity makes it much easier to repeat the desired result when the same job or the same ink is run later. A given manufacturer may have a range of viscosities where his inks have been formulated to perform the best.

ULTRAVIOLET (UV) INKS

UV inks are fundamentally different from water- and solvent-based systems. They don't dry; they *cure* by exposure to high intensity ultraviolet radiation. Pigments are still the colorants, but the resins and diluents that control fluidity are unique. UV ink is a fluid plastic, much like liquid polymer plate material, made up entirely of solids. Since there are no solvents, the ink has no volatiles to evaporate. VOCs are the enemy of clean air and the target for emission control. Therefore there is significant motivation to use UV-curing inks. This is particularly true where traditional solvent systems dominate, specifically in flexo printing on nonporous substrates like films and foils.

The inks contain pigments, resins (acrylic prepolymers before curing), acrylic monomers to control the viscosity, photoinitiators, and additives. The viscosity of the UV ink is determined by the choice of reactive *monomers. Photoinitiators* in the ink facilitate the molecular crosslinking (polymerization) when exposed to high-intensity UV radiation of the correct wavelength. This UV exposure converts the fluid to a solid, virtually in an instant. In actuality, complete cure takes much longer and may never be achieved. In the *free radical* systems that have been the most commonly used, 100% cure is not achieved during the printing and finishing period. Within 24 to 48 hours the inks have cured sufficiently to achieve the required properties of adhesion, rub, and other end uses. The second most common UV chemical approach is the *cationic* system. The UV radiation is used to initiate a chain reaction that continues until the ink is completely cured. The following table lists the components of a typical UV flexo ink.

Component	Portion of Ink
Pigment	15–20%
Resin/Oligomers	40–60%
Liquid Monomers	10–30%
Photoinitiators	5–10%
Additives (incl. waxes)	0.5–2%

Until exposure UV inks remain fluid indefinitely, thus eliminating all printing problems and operator tasks related to ink drying on press, plates, and anilox rolls. Where jobs need to continue to run after a break or a weekend, the press can be left inked, and the run simply continued. Of course dust and light covers must be placed over the printing units to keep the system clean. The problems of dirty print that result from ink drying around edges of images are nonexistent with UV printing. There have been difficulties, however, in achieving solids without pinholes on film substrates. Excessive heat buildup on the substrate, incomplete curing, and odor retained in the product remain issues of concern with UV applications. On the positive side, since there are no volatiles, color consistency and density are improved.

While there are many benefits to UV inks, they are more expensive to purchase and the UV-curing units add cost to the press. Where solvent is replaced, this is offset by the savings associated with environmental requirements. The chemistry of UV inks has been cause for concern due to skin irritation problems. To some extent, as with other chemical systems, this may be isolated to certain individuals. When this sensitivity exists, it is recommended that the person be moved to other work assignments. This has long been the case in many other specific areas including photographic and platemaking operations. Of course wearing plastic gloves is always the recommended practice when handling any chemicals. This eliminates the possibility of health problems caused by direct contact.

END-USE REQUIREMENTS OF FLEXO INK

There are many end-use requirements beyond color and density that a printed ink must achieve. Only the most common will be discussed here.

ADHESION

The most obvious requirement is *adhesion*: sticking to the substrate itself. Inks formulated for printing on paper usually will not adhere to films or other nonabsorbent materials. The ink supplier must know the application before an ink can be supplied to the printer. The basic test of adhesion is the cellophane tape test. This is performed by attaching a strip of specified tape to the printed web and pulling it away. A complete failure would remove the ink entirely, and a total success would leave the ink intact, with no color on the tape. Other tests of adhesion are the scratch test and crinkle test.

RUB

Rub is a test of durability of the printed surface. When packages are shipped it is common for labels to rub against one another. If the labels are marred in any way the product is spoiled. Waxes are among the additives in inks that improve the resistance to rub. Reverse printing is another approach, where the print is applied in reverse to the back side of a clear film substrate. The printed image is viewed through the substrate on the final package. This, of course, puts the ink in contact with the contents. If food, this generally requires the printed web to be laminated to another web, trapping the ink between the two. Laminating inks must also be formulated so they adhere well to both webs and any adhesives that may be used in the process. Heat resistance may also be required.

LIGHTFASTNESS

Lightfastness or resistance to fade is a very common demand of the printing ink. This is mostly determined by pigment selection. Lightfast pigments are normally more expensive than other options, so unnecessary specification of fade resistance might cause excess expense without value. Where the ink will be on a point-of-purchase display for several weeks or months, resistance to sunlight or fluorescent store lighting is a must. If the product is going to be consumed almost immediately, as would a perishable item, there would be little benefit for the additional expense of fade-resistant ink.

Slip Resistance

Another requirement, especially common to corrugated containers, large paperboard cartons, shipping sacks, and multiwall bags is *slide angle*. When stacks of product are moved by conveyors and fork lifts they must remain in a stack as they go up and down ramps and other inclines. This requires a certain amount of resistance to slip. Slip or slide angle, also called *coefficient of friction* (COF), is therefore important. Nonskid materials are often applied with special coatings to meet this requirement. The challenge of providing gloss for visual and protective purposes while also achieving slide angle demands are in opposition to each other. It is common for one package to have two varnishes, one slip resistant on the bottom and top and the other glossy on the primary graphics surfaces.

Product Resistance

Product resistance is another challenge in many packaging applications. Product resistance refers to the ability of the package label to resist exposure to the product inside the package. You recall that most water-based inks are alkaline soluble. What then would happen if the dishwasher detergent dripped down over the label on its bottle? If the ink was a standard water-based product the image on the label would dissolve. The label for this application must be printed with a special alkaline-resistant ink. Of course it could be a solvent or UV ink, but there are special water-based products formulated just for this sort of end use. Other challenging product resistance scenarios include liquor labels, petroleum, and acidic product labels. Product resistance is sometimes achieved by coatings or laminating protective films over the printed substrate.

To understand the scope of other tests, here is a partial list: block resistance, finger twist, Gardner straight-line abrasion, Taber Abraser, crimp seal and sliding iron heat-resistance, ice water resistance, moisture bleed resistance, freeze-thaw resistance, boiling water resistance, smudge resistance, plasticizer bleed resistance, hot wax resistance, and many measures of appearance.

These and numerous other test methods are documented specifically by American Society for Testing and Materials (ASTM), National Association of Printing Ink Manufacturers/National Printing Ink Research Institute (NAPIM/NPIRI), the Committee for Graphic Arts Technologies Standards (CGATS), Technical Association of the Pulp and Paper Industry (TAPPI), and other associations. The Flexographic Technical Association (FFTA) details many tests in its book *Flexography: Principles and Practices.*

Since every ink supplier is a specialist, it is very important for the printer to thoroughly understand all the performance requirements of the printed product and to communicate them to the supplier. Experienced printers know that customers often lack the knowledge to provide all the important information about their product and its use. Therefore the sales or planning departments should seek this information routinely. Providing samples of both the substrate and the contents, in the case of product exposure demands, is the best way to assure success with a new customer's order.

7 SUBSTRATES

There are hundreds of specific substrates printed by the flexo process. This discussion centers on the most common materials and attributes of substrates in general. It deals mostly with those attributes critical to printing. While there are many specific substrates, the printing attributes of this spectrum of materials and surfaces are relatively few. Printing is a surface application of fluid; therefore, the important elements are appearance, including color, gloss, and smoothness, and receptivity to transfer and adhesion. The smoother the surface, the better the image resolution. The whiter and brighter, the better the range and color of the reproduction. The higher the affinity for ink, the easier the printing and the better the adhesion. The substrate is the key determiner of the printing system and thus the key to the appearance, as well as structural performance, of the product. Decisions regarding substrate are determiners of final visual and thus market success.

A generic list of substrates commonly printed flexographically might include paper, paperboard, corrugated, films, laminates, foils, and metal. There are many specific types of papers with different weights and thicknesses, surfaces, strengths, and appearances for their particular end uses. Paperboard is thick paper, used for the spectrum of packaging and specialty applications. Some paperboard is white throughout, but many packaging materials are only white on the surface where appearance is important. If you examine the inside of many cartons you will see the nonvisible side is brown if composed of natural kraft, or gray if made from a mixture of recycled cellulose wood fiber. These materials are often specifically engineered to provide superior strength. For example, much weight is carried by the simple handles on 6-, 12-, and 24-pack drink carriers.

Corrugated board is a structure formed of three liners: the inner and outer surfaces, and the fluted medium in the middle. The outer liner is the one with surface properties so critical to print performance. The corrugated middle layer is called the medium. Its purpose is entirely strength.

Films are commonly referred to as plastics. There are many films, but the most common are polyethylene, polyester, polypropylene, and PVC, known as vinyl. Films may be opaque or clear. Clear films are popular for the "no label look" used on clear glass and plastic containers and windows of cars and businesses. Many films are manufactured with multiple layers. These can be used to get combinations of properties, like strength, barriers to moisture and oxygen, and appearance. Multilayer materials are produced by coextrusion and by lamination. Coextrusion is achieved by heating and feeding different raw materials into separate chambers of the extrusion die. This actually creates the material in a multilayer form. Lamination combines more than one material, joining them by heat or adhesive. Extrusion lamination creates a multilayer structure by extruding a material onto a moving web.

Pressure-sensitive (PS) materials are laminates of a different type. Pressure-sensitive labels are coated with adhesive, peeled from the *liner* carrier, and applied to the product. Figure 7-1 shows the basic structure of pressure-sensitive material. The customer can specify the face stock, which may be virtually any type of paper or film.

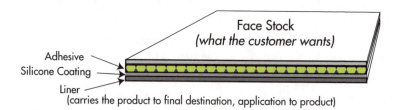

Figure 7-1. The basic structure of pressure-sensitive material.

The adhesive may be very aggressive to stick on dirty or greasy surfaces or very weak to permit easy removal of the label made for temporary use. The liner may be paper or film and is silicone-coated to prevent the adhesive from sticking, thus preventing easy transfer from the liner to the product. The narrow-web industry relies on a broad spectrum of PS substrates to serve needs from industrial to consumer product labels and even stickers popular among the younger set.

Metal, usually in a very thin form called "foil," is popular for its appearance and its opacity. It not only has the sheen and appeal of the metal look, but lends this to a spectrum of transparent colors when printed. It is also commonly used as a cover-up label because it is totally opaque. If a mistake is made in pricing, for example, a label with a layer of foil under the face stock is marked with the corrected price and placed over the error.

PRINTABILITY

All substrates may be categorized as *porous* (absorbent) or *nonporous* (not absorbent). Paper and paperboard substrates are porous. They absorb liquid and are easily printed with any type of ink system. They have a high affinity for liquid. This affinity for ink is known as *surface tension*. High surface tension means good *printability*. Dynes per centimeter is the unit of measurement of surface tension. Substrate printability is rated by applying liquids of calibrated surface tension to the substrate. If the liquid has a surface tension of 40 dynes, and it wets a substrate that would not wet out with a liquid of 38 dynes, the substrate has a surface tension of 40 dynes. Paper has such a high affinity for ink that it generally is not measured. Synthetic films and foils, however, are nonporous. They have a low affinity for liquids. Low surface tension means poor printability. If you wet a plastic bag or aluminum foil and shake it off, most of the water is gone. Unless specially treated for printing, films and foils have surface tensions—dyne levels—in the low thirties. In general surface tension needs to be above 38–40 dynes for printability by standard methods.

Materials having a low affinity for printing inks (low surface tension) can be modified to improve their printability. There are three general ways this is done. The most common method today is corona discharge treatment, which raises the printability by applying a high-voltage, high-frequency electrical charge to the web. Treatment levels fall off with time. Materials treated by the manufacturer for printability may eventually lose their treatment level to the point that they must be retreated before successful printing. Wide-web printers of plastic bags and film laminates often have corona treaters on the infeed sections of their presses, allowing them to raise the dyne level immediately prior to printing. These treaters not only increase the surface area, but also burn away slip agents and dust, which further improves ink transfer and adhesion.

Another common method is flame treatment, whereby the web passes over gas burners which serve to clean and modify the surface resulting in improved printability. The third approach is to apply a printable coating. This is most commonly done by the packagers of specialty pressure-sensitive laminates. The narrow web label manufacturer is called on to print a wide variety of specialty surfaces. The supplier to the narrow-web printer is a converter who buys these materials in large rolls, slits to the narrow-web sizes, applies adhesives to the back, and rewinds with a removable liner. This is the simple structure of a pressure-sensitive label stock. These repackagers commonly apply printable clear coatings so the narrow-web printer can use his normal ink system. Since there is a variety of materials and presses, the use of an in-line treater is often not practical or affordable. Narrow-web printers who specialize in certain nonporous substrate applications do treat or coat in-line to save on costs of special treating and packaging.

SMOOTHNESS

Another major factor affecting print quality is smoothness. The smoother the surface the better the imaging quality. Smooth surfaces require a minimum of ink to achieve required density and solid, uniform coverage. Minimums of ink are always best for clean printing of high-resolution images like fine screens, fine lines, and tiny type. Paper manufacturers are continuously at work to achieve smoother surfaces on their papers to improve printability. The long-time measure of paper smoothness is the Sheffield. Brown kraft paper might have a Sheffield smoothness of 300, while a sheet of coated solid bleached sulfate (SBS)—a standard paperboard used in folding cartons—might measure 50. Coated offset paper for high-quality labels might have a Sheffield of 20. A more recently developed tool is the EMVECO stylus-type smoothness tester. The fine point of the stylus is dragged over the surface. As it responds to the variations in that surface it plots them on a graph and calculates values for frequency and volume. It has been developed to provide a better prediction of printability.

GLOSS

Surfaces are also described by their level of shine. Described as glossy, dull, or matte, these qualities have considerable effect on quality of printed pictures. Smoothness and gloss are created by coating and calendering or polishing. Coatings are most commonly composed of clay and sometimes titanium dioxide. These coatings are used to fill the porous, fibrous surface of paper and paperboard. If they are further polished, they develop a very high sheen or gloss. The more glossy, the higher the apparent density and the longer the range of tones from black to white. These surface attributes also relate to the visibility of smudges and fingerprints. Packaging and consumer items look "used" or handled when such smudges are visible.

WHITENESS AND BRIGHTNESS

An important substrate surface attribute is its whiteness and brightness. These two attributes are closely related but not the same. Whiteness is the degree which the surface reflects all colors of the spectrum. A perfect white would reflect 100% of the additive light primaries red, green, and blue. Brightness is the quantity of the light striking the surface which is reflected. If a surface reflects all the incident light, its brighter than one that reflects only 85%. Reflectance is sometimes enhanced by fluorescing brighteners that reflect UV wavelengths. Since UV is at one point in the spectrum, these brighteners have an adverse effect on whiteness. In general, substrates that are very bright also tend to be very white. Whiteness and brightness along with smoothness and gloss all are required for the highest quality color reproduction.

PICK RESISTANCE

The last surface attributes of particular importance to the flexo printer are cleanliness and strength or *pick resistance*. Lint and dust come from loose fibers in paper and clay coatings that are brittle and shatter when slit, either at the paper mill or in-line during printing and converting. These particles are frequently picked up by the flexo plate and show on repeating images as *dirty print* and voids or white specs. Certain substrates are very subject to these problems. Thin ink films show these problems even more than thicker films. For this reason some corrugated printers prefer printing more ink than ideal print quality would require. The best solution, short of cleaner material manufacture, is the installation of cleaners in-line on the printing press. Varieties of electrostatic, mechanical, and vacuum devices are available for this purpose. Figure 7-2 shows the same sheet of corrugated board printed with a low volume and with a more suitable volume of ink. The difference in appearance demonstrates the critical requirement of either cleaning or covering dusty board.

Pick resistance is the strength of the surface, which keeps it from being pulled apart by the tack or stickiness of the ink. Since flexo uses a liquid ink, compared to offset and letterpress, tack is very low. This, and the ability to adjust viscosity, makes flexo a superior process to print on low-strength surfaces. This is why flexo is the choice for tissues and paper toweling, both of which are low in surface strength.

THICKNESS

The thickness of substrates is another attribute that can be of considerable importance in printing. Thickness of paper is specified in *basis weight*, the weight in pounds of 500 sheets of the *basic size*. Basic size is determined by the most common use of the paper. For example, bond or writing paper is most commonly used in 8½×11-in. sheets cut from the standard or basic size of 17×22 in. One of the most common weights is 16-lb. bond. This means that 500 sheets of 17×22-in. paper weigh 16 pounds. 24-lb. bond paper is a thicker gauge, and 13-lb. bond is very thin. When a label printer orders pressure-sensitive label stock, the basis weight of the face stock and the liner must be specified.

Paperboard, on the other hand, is specified by gauge in points or thousandths of an inch. 10-pt. "board" is 0.010 in. (ten thousandths) thick. Small folding cartons may be as thin as 10-pt., while large cartons for packaging heavy objects may be 24–30 pt. (0.024–0.030 in.) thick. Linerboard used to make corrugated board is specified in still another method, weight in pounds per thousand square feet, lb/msf.

Corrugated board is a structure. Its thickness is specified by flute design. The most common board for transporting consumer goods is B-flute. The boxes at the grocery store, for example, are B-flute (0.104 in. thick). Bigger boxes that carry heavier objects may be C-flute (0.146 in. thick), or A-flute (0.165 in. thick). Small containers may be E-, F- or N-flute (0.050 in., 0.030–0.045 in., and 0.015–0.025 in. thick respectively). The thicker the board the larger the space between the flute tips and the more *washboard* the surface. When printing on C-flute it is common for the print to have dark lines along the flute tips where the board is thicker and harder. The thinner the corrugated board the more level the surface and the less likely there will be objectionable flute marks in the print. The thin boards are very popular for retail packaging in warehouse and club stores. Due to the small fluting, they accept very high-quality graphics with screens commonly as fine as 100–120 lines per inch and even

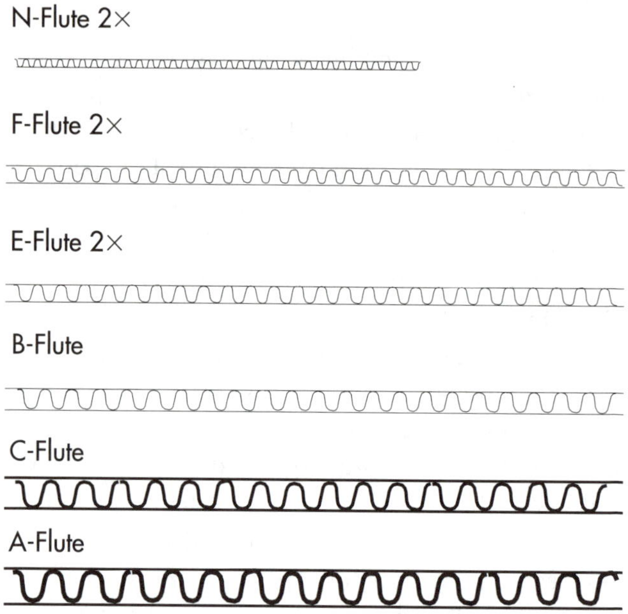

N-Flute 2×

F-Flute 2×

E-Flute 2×

B-Flute

C-Flute

A-Flute

Figure 7-2. Several different flute boards.

finer at times. This permits flexo printing directly on boards having high-holdout liners at quality levels to rival litho labels, which must be applied in a separate operation.

Figure 7-2 shows the actual size of A-, B-, C-, E-, F-, and N-flute boards. This makes it easy to see how corrugated converters would be seeking markets that have been folding carton or paperboard markets in the past. Corrugated has superior strength, especially when stacking packages, compared to paperboard. Figure 7-3 also shows why the thin corrugated board is now being printed on sheetfed offset presses configured for heavy paperboard printing applications.

8 THE PLATE

The plate is the second of flexo's two hearts, the first being the anilox roll. Its resilience permits applications on the widest variety of substrates. The many imaging approaches enable its application on a spectrum of images, including continuous patterns. Plate materials permit imaging with all types of inks. Thin plates and shallow relief provide capability crossing the spectrum of screen resolutions. Developments continue to increase the capability of the process and its competitiveness with other more mature printing methods.

The resilient, displaceable plate is what enables flexographic printing to be applied to such a wide variety of materials. The plate works like the offset blanket in its ability to conform to irregularities in substrates. Therefore it is not limited to smooth substrates as are letterpress and gravure, with their hard plate surfaces. This same positive quality also has drawbacks. The ability to add squeeze when the plate has a low spot (to get that spot to print) is what causes the common problem of excess impression and the unsightly ring around images. In less forgiving processes, a bad plate is immediately replaced and thus poor quality is not printed. Careful quality checks of flexographic plates are, therefore, essential to top-quality printing that compares favorably with any process. Excellent flexographic printing is produced routinely because of the capability of the resilient plate. Top performing printers have the most stringent quality assurance practices in place.

The terminology used to describe the plate is detailed in Figure 8-1. The *face* is the image that prints. It must be smooth and have sharp edges. The *shoulders* will be as straight as possible where they

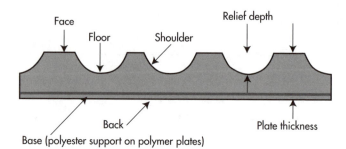

Figure 8-1. Diagram of the physical parts of the flexographic printing plate.

meet the face. Ideally they will angle out from the face to provide support to fine lines and small halftone dots. The *floor* is the non-image area. The distance between floor and face is *relief depth* and is critical to the relief principle. Contrary to standard practice, large relief depths are unnecessary as proven by the newspaper printers and leaders in narrow-web printing, both of whom print with relief depths of as little as 0.015 in. The *back* or *base* of the plate, in the case of photopolymers, is a polyester sheet and provides dimensional stability. It may also be metal as with many newspaper plates and plates mounted to cylinders magnetically. Rubber plates, with limited exceptions, have no stable backing. The *total plate thickness* is determined by the space between the cylinder and the pitch line of the gear where the transfer of image to substrate is achieved. Thin plates are between 0.025 in. and 0.045 in., and are found most commonly in news and narrow-web label applications. Others are slowly moving in this direction. Plates between 0.067 in. and 0.125 in. are very common in most industry segments, with the exception of corrugated. There it is still common to find plates between 0.150 in. and 0.250 in. Trends in almost all flexographic applications are to thinner plates, which are found to hold better resolution and print with less gain.

PLATE MAKEUP

All flexographic printing plates are either made of rubber or photopolymer. The original plate material was rubber. It was the only available plate material until photosensitized polymers were introduced in 1973 by DuPont. The entire printing system was based on a rubber plate and its ink transfer properties. The early polymer plates were measured by their performance in comparison to rubber. There were a variety of formulations of rubber developed for their specific performance properties.

Any flexographic plate, whether rubber or photopolymer, must first have good *printability*, accepting and transferring ink between the anilox roll and the substrate. Printability also requires *resilience* or the ability to rebound immediately following anilox contact and again after impression. Resilience enables the plate to accept ink and transfer it the same way at whatever speeds are required by the printer. The plate must also resist the solvents in the inks, meaning it must not swell or change in hardness, measured in durometer units. It must resist deterioration from wear caused by repeated impressions against the anilox and the substrate being printed.

Plate performance requires levelness or uniformity over the entire image area. Plates that vary in thickness require overimpression from the anilox to receive ink. This pushes ink over the shoulders in the high areas. This ink prints dirty images when impressed to the substrate. These same areas are overimpressed to the substrate, which alone will cause print gain in both line and screened areas. Foam mounting tape provides significant forgiveness for variability in plate thickness, but there is no substitute for tight tolerances in plate thickness and uniformity. Durometer (the hardness of the plate) is also very important. The more irregular and/or porous the substrate, the softer the plate material. Plates of 25–35 durometer on the Shore A scale are used for corrugated board where conforming to the washboard-like surface and rough paper liner is required. Plates of 55–60 durometer are the norm, and harder plates are often used on very hard, smooth substrates where the highest image resolutions are achievable.

RUBBER PLATEMAKING PROCEDURE

Rubber plates are made by a series of steps (see Figure 8-2, pp. 108–110, for the production flow) starting with a negative, specially

1. Negatives used to image photo resist on pattern plate.

2. Pattern plate is developed to remove unexposed resist.

5. Relief pattern plate is proofed.

6. Matrix is impressed from pattern plate.

Figure 8-2. Production flow of the rubber flexographic platemaking process.

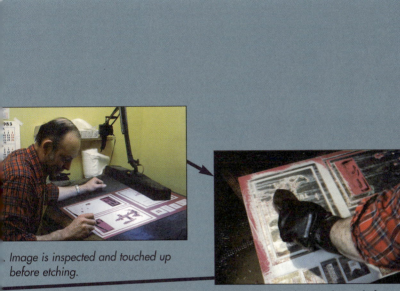

. Image is inspected and touched up before etching.

4. Plate is etched to produce relief. Remaining resist is removed.

. Rubber is molded/vulcanized from matrix.

8. Finished plate is inspected for correct thickness and relief.

sized and distorted for the specific rubber being used. Since the rubber molding process includes two steps where heat is involved, the changes in size caused by heating and cooling materials must be compensated. There are different ways to account for size change. In preparation of conventional art the work is prepared oversized by the amount that the materials will shrink. The other way is to prepare art

exactly the desired size and enlarge it in the imaging process for the shrinking that will occur as the materials cool. Compensation for wrap distortion (elongation) is handled as always, by shortening the image in the direction "around" the plate cylinder.

Original art or electronic files are prepared normally for rubber plate production. There is an additional *bearer* produced that surrounds the art area, normally just outside the trim lines for the product. This bearer, often referred to as a "barrier," serves as a holding line for the materials being molded. It keeps the heated, plastic-like material from flowing away from the image in the path of least resistance. It is generally used to display job numbers and other production information since it goes all the way through platemaking until being cut off prior to mounting. It is an easy way to keep track of the job during prepress operations.

The negative is exposed onto the light-sensitive coating of the metal or photopolymer pattern plate. A variety of materials including magnesium, lead type, copper, and hard photopolymer are imaged to make the original pattern plate. Magnesium is the most commonly used pattern plate material. Hard photopolymer is gaining in use because of its preferred interaction with the environment and the workplace.

The pattern plate is processed into a hard, letterpress-type relief plate. This becomes the "original" relief plate that will be duplicated in rubber for use in flexographic printing. Metal pattern plates are developed after exposure to remove the acid-resistant coating. The plate is etched with acid to the desired depth. This determines the relief depth of the final rubber plate. Then the plate is inspected and flaws are removed to prepare it for making the *matrix*, a mold.

The rest of the rubber platemaking process takes place using a precision vulcanizer, or molding press. Figure 8-3 shows a vulcanizer and a diagram of its key parts.

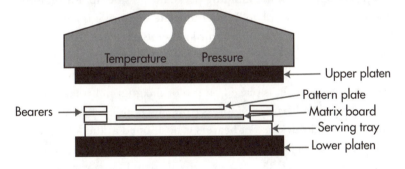

Figure 8-3. A vulcanizer (top) and a diagram of its key parts (bottom).

Matrix board, sometimes called bakelite, is cut to size, brushed to be sure it is free of foreign particles, and inserted face up into the molding press. The pattern plate is placed on top, image side down, and pressed under heat and pressure into the matrix board. Thickness control bearers are placed along both sides of the molding surface, called the serving tray, to control the thickness of the matrix. The matrix is a thermal plastic resin and cellulose material. The resin provides a smooth hard surface for molding the rubber plate. The matrix is molded to a specified floor thickness, the thickness between the face of the image and the back of the matrix board. Figure 8-4 shows the assembly of pattern plate, matrix, cover sheet, and the thickness control bearers.

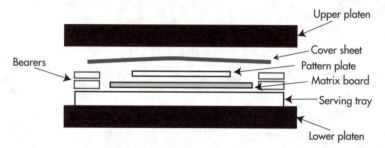

Figure 8-4. *The assembly of pattern plate, matrix, and cover sheet, and the thickness of control bearers.*

After checking the floor thickness and uniformity of the matrix, it is placed back into the molding press, image side up, for molding the duplicate rubber plate. It is a duplicate because it is a copy of the pattern plate. In fact it is a third-generation plate, the first and second generations being the pattern plate and the matrix. The gum, which becomes rubber when vulcanized, is placed over the matrix. A cover sheet is placed on top of the gum to protect the upper platen of the molding press from any buildup of material. The exact total thickness of bearers is positioned at the left and right of the serving tray and the entire assembly is inserted into the heated plate molder. The bearers are calculated exactly to determine the thickness of the plate. The heat and pressure from the molding press soften the gum while hydraulic pressure pushes it into every part of the matrix. The assembly of matrix and gum is held for a specific time at 307°F until it is completely vulcanized, changed to rubber.

Quality checks, explained in detail below, often reveal slight irregularities in total plate thickness and uniformity. Small amounts of unevenness in rubber plates are often corrected by a grinding procedure. The plate is positioned with its face against a precision drum, held down by tape. A "sanding" roller, turning at high RPMs, is brought into contact with the back of the plate as its drum rotates slowly. As long as very light grinding is employed, it can be used to improve print quality. It is common, however, for excess grinding to cause severe cupping under the plate surface and result in the edges printing first, showing a pronounced ring around the images.

PHOTOPOLYMER PLATEMAKING PROCEDURES

As the name implies, photopolymer plates are light-sensitive, and the platemaking procedures employ multiple exposures to light to determine their relief depth and shoulder angles. Figure 8-5 (pg. 114) provides images of the sheet photopolymer production flow. The raw materials are either in a liquid or a precast sheet form. Figure 8-6 describes the sheet type of plate, available in a wide variety of sizes from small (12×15 in.) up to 50×80 in. and possibly larger today; change is constant.

There are many sizes and types of exposure devices. The diagram in Figure 8-7 is just one typical exposure system. The procedure for exposure and processing is simple. The plate material has a base and a face side. The base side is determined by the firmly attached polyester sheet. This provides the plate with dimensional stability. The base resists size changes and cannot be stretched during handling, particularly mounting. The first exposure is made through the base. Its duration determines floor thickness. Since total plate thickness is a specification of the sheet plate as it is supplied, floor thickness is the determiner of *relief depth*. Relief depth is a major factor in determining print quality. The longer the back exposure, the thicker the floor. Back exposure also affects the length of the face exposure.

The face side of the plate also has a polyester sheet, but it is easily peeled off prior to imaging. *Face exposure* is the imaging exposure made through the negative held in contact by a vacuum and a flexi-

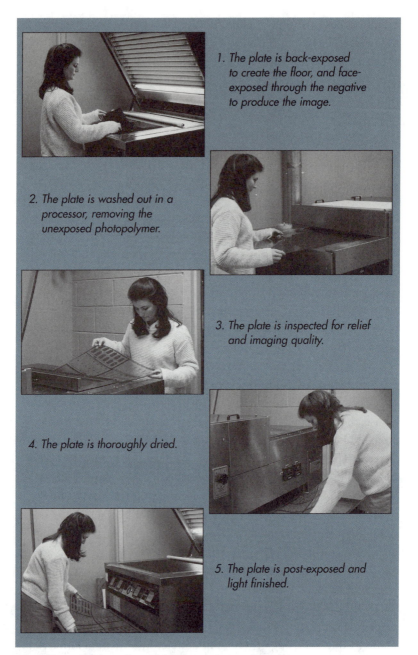

1. The plate is back-exposed to create the floor, and face-exposed through the negative to produce the image.

2. The plate is washed out in a processor, removing the unexposed photopolymer.

3. The plate is inspected for relief and imaging quality.

4. The plate is thoroughly dried.

5. The plate is post-exposed and light finished.

Figure 8-5. Production flow of the photopolymer platemaking process.

Removable cover sheet

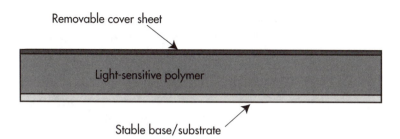

Light-sensitive polymer

Stable base/substrate

Figure 8-6. The sheet type of plate, which is available in a wide variety of sizes.

Face exposure lamps

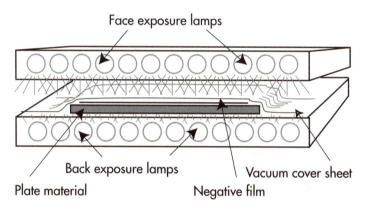

Back exposure lamps   Vacuum cover sheet

Plate material   Negative film

Figure 8-7. Schematic of a typical exposure system.

ble drawdown sheet. The length of the face exposure determines the *shoulder angle,* which controls support of the image. Fine lines will be wavy if there is insufficient face exposure. Very small highlight dots will fail to image or be weak and move during impression without enough face exposure. Stochastic images require more face exposure to image the highlight "spots" since they are farther apart, somewhat independent of adjacent spots. Too much face exposure causes excess dot gain, particularly in highlights and quartertones. Figure 8-8 illustrates the effect of face exposure time on images.

Once the plate is exposed the material has been rendered stable or insoluble. The unexposed material is still a soluble monomer. It is processed by simply dissolving in an appropriate solvent or detergent. The plate is also scrubbed with brushes during washout to

Short face exposure produces straight, vertical shoulders. This may result in too little support of the image areas, especially small lines and dots.

Long face exposure produces more shoulder angle and better support of fine detail. Excessive face exposure results in print gain and even a loss of relief within image areas.

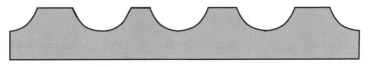

Figure 8-8. The effect of face exposure time on images..

speed the process by removing the unexposed material as it is dissolved. Solvent-washed plates require a blotting step to assure all solvent and plate material are removed from the printing surface. This is a simple but critical part of the platemaking process. Any foreign material left on the face of the plate causes noticeable defects in the printed image.

Solvent-washed plate material absorbs some of the solvent, and time is required while drying for this material to escape from the plate. Detergent-washed plate materials don't absorb liquid and thus require less time for drying. Dryers provide hot air and exhaust for rapid removal of moisture and vapors.

After the plate is processed and dried, it requires *post exposure* to cure all remaining unexposed material and *finishing* to eliminate a tackiness on its surface. While there are alternative methods, finishing is usually done by a UV light finishing process. (Figure 8-9 illustrates the process of making a sheet plate.)

LIQUID POLYMER PLATES

Liquid polymer plates are made following exactly the same exposure and processing steps. The difference is that the parts of the

1. Negatives are placed onto the glass

2. A cover sheet is placed over the negatives

3. The resin is cast and the plate exposed

4. The exposed plate is removed from the platemaker. The plate is washed out, postexposed, and finished similar to a sheet plate.

Figure 8-9. The process of making a liquid polymer plate.

plate come as separate items to the liquid platemaking department. The base, or substrate, of the plate is a sheet of polyester. One side has a matte surface to assure its firm attachment to the polymer resin. The polymer is in liquid resin form comparable to honey in appearance and consistency. There is a thin plastic cover sheet used to keep the resin off the negatives during exposure.

Figure 8-10 shows the platemaking machine. It is the exposure unit as well as the plate construction system. The plate is completely manufactured on this single machine from its raw materials.

Figure 8-10. Platemaking machine

While there are many features of liquid platemaking systems, the basic process is the same. The operator positions the negatives, emulsion up, on the lower glass which is cleaned before every plate is made. A very thin cover sheet is pulled over the negatives and drawn down with vacuum. The operator inserts a sheet of substrate into the carriage of the machine and checks the supply of resin. While this can be manually poured into the resin reservoir, it is usually supplied automatically from a pressurized manifold system. The carriage is activated. It moves across the negatives, pouring a metered quantity of resin and simultaneously laying down the polyester base of the plate. As soon as the carriage is clear of the plate area, the top of the machine is closed and vacuum is applied between the top and bottom glasses. This is done to assure the plate completely fills the space between the two glasses. This space is the critical plate thickness and determines plate uniformity required for quality flexographic printing. The exposures are made. First the back exposure lamp comes on. As with a sheet system, this is timed to establish the floor thickness (and relief depth) while also increasing the sensitivity of the resin to the face exposure. While the back exposure is being made, the face exposure is started from the bottom lamps. This exposure is made through the negatives and determines the imaging and the shoulder support of the plate.

When the exposures are complete the unit is opened and the plate is removed. The cover sheet is discarded and unexposed resin reclaimed. The plate is placed into the processor washout unit; the processor washes out all the unexposed resin using a heated detergent and water solution. Once washed out, the plate is rinsed and moved to the finishing unit where it is postexposed and finished simultaneously, in a special solution to remove the tackiness and to leave the plate ready to be used once it has been dried. Drying has only to remove water from the surface since there is no absorption into the plate.

Liquid platemaking departments almost always reclaim a significant amount of the unexposed resin before the plate is washed out. This is done by placing it on a vertical surface where, after removal of the cover sheet, a high-velocity air knife is passed down over the plate causing the unexposed resin to roll off into a catch basin. This resin is used again in the platemaking process, saving both material cost and pollution of the washout and subsequent wastewater.

Liquid polymer plates permit a special capping procedure that can improve reproduction on certain substrates and types of graphics. Very simply, before the liquid is cast over the negatives, a special capping resin is often manually coated onto the cover sheet. This resin is sometimes harder and provides a better image transfer while maintaining the plate resilience with the rest of the normal resin applied by the automatic system. This cap has less shoulder angle at the face of the plate, resulting in cleaner print and thus reduced dot gain. Some caps are the same hardness, but provide different image transfer properties.

DIGITAL FLEXOGRAPHIC PLATES

Currently there are several varieties of direct-to-plate, or digitally imaged flexographic plates. As with all printing processes, the motivation is to eliminate film imaging costs and improve throughput. Of course, improvements in quality are also expected.

The first direct-to-plate process was laser engraving rubber. In this process gum is vulcanized and precisely ground to final plate thickness. It is then mounted to a drum and rotated in front of a CO_2 laser. The nonimage area is burned away leaving the image in relief and the plate ready for mounting (see Figure 8-11). Laser-engraved rubber plates have precisely controlled shoulder angle, and resolution as high as 120-line halftone screens can be produced. One of the most appealing applications of this technology is the production of continuous-pattern images. Conventional plates always leave a gap or line where the two ends of the plate come together on the cylinder. Continuous patterns are laser-engraved onto rubber-covered rollers. Rubber is vulcanized to roller bases and ground to the exact repeat length. This roller is then laser-imaged. Gift wrap and wall covering often require uninterrupted patterns, and laser imaging is a popular solution. This process also eliminates any plate mounting and the cost of potential register flaws that go with mounting.

The second direct-to-plate system simply substitutes a polymer plate for the rubber and, as above, images the polymerized material by laser burning away the unwanted polymer in nonimage areas.

The other two direct digital imaging approaches are digital-photographic hybrids. They both employ digital masking of light and conventional photographic exposure and washout processing. The first of these was first introduced by DuPont at DRUPA 95. It uses a laser to ablate (remove) a mask (black or other light stop-ping coating), which is applied on top of a conventional photo-polymer plate. The plate material is supplied with the light-stopping mask. It is mounted onto a drum in the laser ablation unit and rotated in front of the laser. The laser removes the light mask leav-ing the image area open to pass light during the exposure step. The plate now has a negative built into it. It is placed on the stan-dard exposure unit and given the same exposure as used on con-ventional plates. The benefit to the process is, of course, that there is no need to produce film. The lack of a negative does eliminate any issues of dust from film and halation due to contact problems, so quality is clearly improved. Without the negative and drawdown sheet, diffusion of light is also eliminated and, thus, resolution improved. This is particularly valuable in the lightest highlights. As with most new technologies, the early applications show little if any financial benefit. There has been little or no difference in throughput with single laser machines. Market realities should lead to future economic benefits for the consumer flexo printer. This

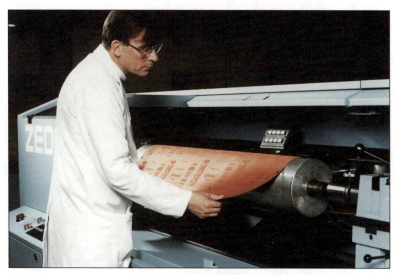

Figure 8-11. Operator examining a laser-engraved rubber plate.

digital approach is also used to image photopolymer on sleeves providing a "seamless" plate if necessary. This, of course, eliminates all plate mounting and the register issues that often result.

The third direct digital approach is the same as used by screen printers to apply graphics to photographic screens for many years. It employs an inkjet imager that applies a light-stopping mask to the sheet flexo plate. Once imaged, the plate is exposed and processed as any other sheet-type plate. This system is far less expensive but also limited in its early form by the capability of inkjet imaging.

9 PLATE MOUNTING

egardless of the system of plates and cylinders, the register and impression are determined by this phase of production. Presses have lateral (across) and circumferential (around) register. All the accuracy within the image is determined by prepress, particularly plate mounting. There are tools available today to make this step accurate and productive. There are still many, however, using older techniques which require greater allowance for register tolerance. All involved in the production process need to be aware of the process capability being employed on the job at hand. This is just one more reason for making the project a team effort, involving all along the production chain to achieve the best possible results for the customer.

The plate, regardless of its origin, is part of a system. This system includes the plate, the stickyback or other mounting medium, and the cylinder, sleeve, or carrier sheet onto which it is mounted. Today there are many ways to assemble this system, and new approaches are being developed. The fundamentals, however, are constant, valuable, and prerequisite to understanding the latest approaches.

PLATE MOUNTING FUNDAMENTALS

The plate mounting process is simply the precise positioning of the plate in the x and y axes. If the plates are mounted perfectly square, the running adjustments on the press permit easy registration on the run. Unlike offset lithographic presses, flexo presses with plates mounted directly to cylinders or sleeves permit no angle adjust-

Plate centerline not parallel to cylinder centerline

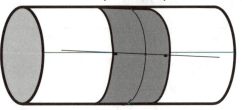

Plate centerline parallel to cylinder centerline

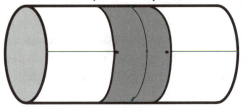

Multiple plates square to cylinder centerline; plates are staggered to prevent bounce as plates go on and off impression.

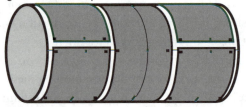

Figure 9-1. The plate mounting process is the precise positioning of the plate in the x and y axes. Plates must be positioned squarely to the plate cylinder.

ments. They must be mounted perfectly square (Figure 9-1). In the case of corrugated and a few other exceptions where plates are mounted to carrier sheets, angle adjustments are possible. Making angle adjustments is, however, always cumbersome and costly.

When jobs are run more than one-up, plates are either made in single pieces for each color of the entire job or one label at a time. In other words, a three-color job runs three images across and two around the cylinder could be plated with just three plates, each containing six images (3 across × 2 around), or it could be plated with 18 individual plates.

In the past flexo plates were always done as individuals, 18 plates for this scenario. This required very skilled mounters and often more than a shift just to mount the job. It also meant there were 18 potential mounting errors for this simple job. Today, with large film output devices and platemakers, a job of this description would more likely be prepared with one large plate for each color. Now there are only three positioning tasks. There are also precision tools available to assure accurate location of each plate. The cost of plate mounting has moved from labor to tools and technology. This permits much shorter times to press and far less press downtime for repositioning plates that were poorly mounted.

STICKYBACK TAPE

Most plates are mounted to the cylinder or carrier by two-sided tape called stickyback. Stickyback comes in selected thicknesses, densities, and hardnesses. Some stickybacks simply adhere the plate and may be as thin as 0.002 in. Other stickybacks are thicker, most commonly 0.015 in. and 0.020 in. thick. These are either rigid or cushioned. Cushion stickyback is a foam material that aids impression uniformity. Consistent thickness of stickyback is critical to the job. Variation in stickyback is the same as variation in the plate thickness. Much research has been done to understand the ideal stickyback and plate combinations for selected types of images. The mounting tape has a major effect on the print quality of the product. To oversimplify, harder tape is best for solids and soft for fine screens. Since there is considerable interaction among graphics, inks, and substrates, the optimum choice is generally given serious thought. This is an area where top printers often find that one size does not fit all.

PLATE ALIGNMENT CONCEPTS

For the purpose of this text, all plate alignment systems will be grouped into three categories: optical, register pins, or videoscopes

Figure 9-2. A simple visual approach to mounting a plate.

and microtargets. These are not clean divisions because some employ more than one concept.

Optical devices rely on simple visual alignment of the position marks on the plate with grids or layout lines. The simplest optical approach relies on scribed lines in the cylinder itself. The mounter simply lines up the vertical and horizontal center marks of the plate with the marks scribed into the cylinder. Simple? Yes; remember, all that is required is a plate mounted squarely on a cylinder. Other optical approaches enable the plate to be positioned squarely on a sheet or table and then transferred to the cylinder. Figure 9-2 illustrates one simple visual approach where the plate is aligned with a grid.

Devices called *optical mounter-proofers* have been used for many years. Two such mounters known by the names of their inventors, Harley and Mosstype (for Earl Harley and Samuel Moss), employ mirrors to enable the operator to line up the marks on the plate with a drafted position layout on the impression cylinder of the device. The operator uses the drafting features of the machine to draw out the press/web layout. Then the operator inserts a print cylinder for one color into the machine and attaches a gear that locks in the "around the cylinder" position. If the plates are to be mounted three-around, after each plate is positioned the cylinder is turned exactly one third the circumference to mount the next plate. Each plate is positioned to hit exactly on the drafted lines. To check register, the plates are inked and an impression made onto the drafted sheet. After each cylinder is mounted it is inked and proofed, resulting in a paper-and-ink proof of the entire mounted job. The proof normally is checked both in mounting and the press department where it goes along with the cylinders for the pressrun. Optical mounter-proofers require very skilled operators. It could take more than one shift to mount a six-color, complex job where many plates are involved. *Bieffebi* is another optical mounter-proofer based on the same principles.

Today these same "mounter-proofers" are often retrofitted with pin register systems or videoscopes to permit more critical alignment with far less skill and time. There are several retrofit options that permit modernizing older, yet still-valuable mounter-proofers. Figure 9-3 shows a typical mounter-proofer.

Figure 9-3. A typical mounter-proofer.

PIN REGISTRATION SYSTEMS

The graphic arts industry has employed pins to align images for decades. Prior to sheet polymer plate materials, the use of register pins had to stop with the final film in the flexographic process. Today there are approaches using pins to line up images with plates and plates with cylinders and carrier sheets. Pin registration of images on film to the plate is achieved by drilling sheet photo-polymer plate material with holes matched to holes in the final films. After back-exposing the plate material, the pins are placed through the holes and used to position the film during face expo-sure, just as is routinely done with litho plates. These same register holes are then used for mounting onto the cylinders.

It is more common for plates to be made without regard to image position and then drilled for plate mounting with pins. This approach involves locating the imaged plate precisely using micro-scopes and tiny microtargets built into the image. Once positioned the plate is drilled for mounting. The plate is then located on pins, sometimes right on the cylinder or carrier. Pins are sometimes part of a mounting device used to transfer the plate to the cylinder. Figure 9-4 illustrates the concept of employing pins to position the plate for mounting. On the top the plate is precisely aligned and drilled with holes for register pins. On the bottom the plate is positioned on pins as it is transferred to the stickyback on the print cylinder.

VIDEO MICROSCOPES

Video microscopes represent the third approach. While these same tools are also used in some pin register systems, this concept by-pass-es drilling and simply permits precise positioning of the plate over the cylinder/carrier and attaching without any additional action. A pair of microtargets are imaged into all the plates. The mounting system has at least two video microscopes. If multiple plates are being mounted, there must be two scopes for each plate position. The plate is precisely located so the video crosshair is exactly on the microtarget. Once located, the plate is brought into contact with the stickyback. The position of the scopes is locked for all colors being

Figure 9-4. The pin-registration concept. The plate is drilled (top), then pinned to the cylinder (bottom).

mounted and documented for future mounting, or for remounting should a plate be damaged on press. This is a very accurate and fast approach to mounting. It is so reliable that many printers no longer

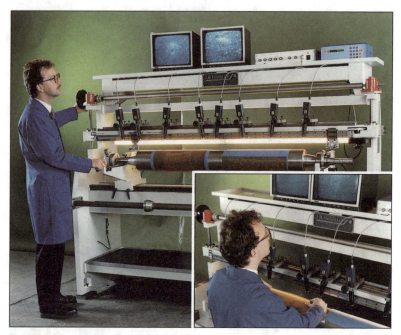

Figure 9-5. Heaford videoscope plate register system.

demand a proof from the mounted plates. This approach to mounting also has a perfect fit to modern digital prepress, which makes exact location of microtargets a routine part of the workflow. Figure 9-5 shows a Heaford videoscope plate register system. At the right the operator positions a plate while watching the monitor to see when it is perfectly aligned.

PLATE CYLINDERS

There are three general cylinder approaches from which flexographers may choose when building their plate system. (See Figure 9-6.) They may be *integral, demountable* (small narrow-web examples shown), or lightweight *sleeves*. Integral plate cylinders are the most expensive and, arguably, probably the most accurate and precise over their lifespan. The one-piece cylinder is made for a single repeat length, circumference, and has precision journals to hold gears and

Figure 9-6. Three different cylinder types: integral (top), demountable (middle), and sleeve (bottom).

bearings. They are often unique to a given press. Since they are one piece, they have no tolerances for assembly and are subjected to less labor activity, meaning less chance for accidental damage.

Demountable cylinder systems consist of a shaft or mandrel, and metal sleeves machined to specific repeat lengths. These steel or aluminum sleeves are installed for the specific job, and corresponding gears and bearings are installed at the time of mounting. Therefore only one set of shafts with precision bearing and gear journals is required for a wide variety of repeat lengths on a press. This system is the dominant approach in narrow-web applications.

Lightweight sleeves are a solution for the larger sizes of presses where the costs of cylinders are especially high and where the demount system still requires a lifting apparatus for handling. Jobs can be set up for mounting directly to the sleeve, or the sleeve may be covered with vulcanized and ground rubber to provide desired resilience qualities and to permit a range of repeat lengths from just a few mandrel diameters. Figure 9-7 illustrates how a single sleeve and mandrel size can accommodate a range of repeat lengths.

To run light sleeves the press is equipped with hollow plate cylinder mandrels fitted with compressed air fixtures. The sleeve is slipped over the end of the mandrel by hand. Air is applied to the mandrel and passes through small holes positioned along the entire length of the mandrel. This air provides sufficient pressure to expand the sleeve just enough to be pushed by hand all the way onto the mandrel. When the air pressure is removed the sleeve is too tight to be moved. After use the mandrel is again pressurized and the sleeve is removed. Very large sleeves are still light enough to be handled manually, making their use and storage easy, and requiring the least in materials handling systems.

Sleeves offer a variety of other benefits for the creative. Among the most obvious advantages is the ability to leave jobs mounted for running on any one of a variety of presses. Jobs can be left mounted for reruns since less cost is tied up with cylinder inventory. This also results in substantial savings in plate mounting and in remaking plates damaged during removal and storage. Jobs can be mixed

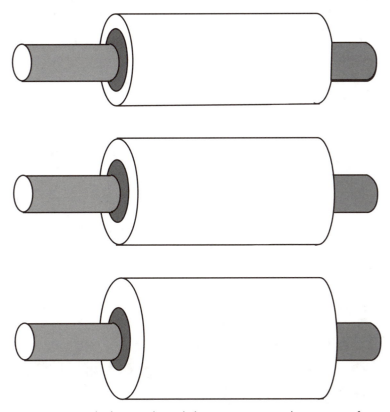

Figure 9-7. A single sleeve and mandrel size can accommodate a range of repeat lengths.

on a pressrun by mounting more than one narrow sleeve on a mandrel. Where a converter runs repeat and standard items, this makes it possible to offer short runs without unrealistic waste of press capacity. They are also popular where continuous digitally imaged pattern rolls are used. The sleeve allows much less expensive inventory of patterns for repeating jobs and costs of handling and shipping to the laser engraver are substantially reduced. Sleeves are also a convenient vehicle for trying out new plate thicknesses without investing in an inventory of cylinders. Since they can be easily built up to various thicknesses they are useful as tools for process improvement.

10 THE PRESSES

The competitive edge for flexography over other processes is generally the versatility of the press combined with variable repeat printing. High print quality is a given requirement. Efficiency in production, particularly converting, gets the job for one printer or converter over the other. Creativity in the marketing and planning departments is critical to business development; all players in the production chain willing to try the unusual are bound to be part of a winning team. Some of the most elegant solutions today employ mixed printing processes as well as the creative converting achievements. Customers are in love with results and not printing processes, so the printers who combine the best of all their options will be likely to win in the overall competition. Offset, screen, gravure, letterpress, flexo, and digital each do certain things better than others. Look for more and more creativity in picking and mixing the best for still better solutions and happier customers. The press is where it all is assembled as a manufacturing system.

A printing press is a device that physically brings all the elements of the process together. It feeds and controls the substrate through impression with the plate in the printing station. It moves the substrate and freshly inked image through the dryers. It has controls to adjust and maintain the side-to-side position of the substrate through the print station. It provides for vertical and circumferential adjustment of the image at each print station. It provides for tension control throughout the path from the unwind to the rewind. Many presses include converting units to slit the web, diecut patterns, laminate additional webs to the printed substrate, and sheet and stack products. It is common to have other printing stations such as screen printing for overprinting graphics or coatings. There may be embossing, numbering, or even digital print stations for variable information or graphics.

PRINCIPAL TYPES OF PRINTING PRESSES

There are three fundamental styles of press design, and they may be found as flexo, litho, gravure, letterpress, or screen printing presses. It is becoming more common every year for presses to have more than one process, taking advantage of what each process does best. The three press designs are *in-line, stack,* and *common* or *central impression (CI).* Figure 10-1 diagrams the three press designs.

Presses are further categorized as narrow web, wide web, and sheetfed. Industry segments tend to use specialized applications of certain press designs. For example, the tag and label manufacturers tend to use more in-line press designs for flexographic applications. The printers of flexible packaging favor CI presses because they provide superior control of flexible, lightweight films used in packaging snack foods, frozen vegetables, and many other products. Stack presses are often used by the multiwall bag industry where more stable substrates permit adequate control at substantially less cost than CI designs. The printers of corrugated board use sheetfed, in-line presses. These presses are uniquely engineered to control very heavy corrugated board and apply graphics to relatively irregular surfaces compared to other applications.

IN-LINE PRESSES

The in-line design has certain advantages over others. Since all units are mounted to the floor, operators can move from one station to the other and make adjustments to print without awkward physical efforts. It is easier than other designs to view the web while adjusting the print. Another advantage of the in-line design is the natural modularity of the parts. Adding units to increase the capacity simply requires making space and inserting the new stations. The drawback of the in-line press is the amount of material within

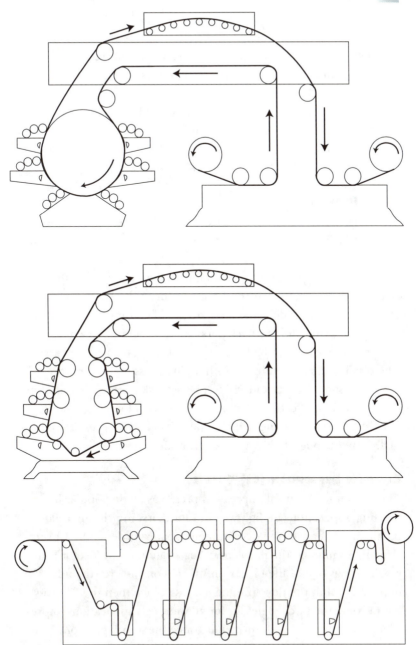

Figure 10-1. Three different types of printing press. (Top) Common-impression cylinder; (middle) stack; and (bottom) inline.

the press at all times. There might be as much as 150 feet of material between the unwind and rewind of a six-color narrow-web press. It is very common to have narrow-web presses with as many as ten colors. Presses like those used to print lottery tickets may have many more units. This means that considerable material may be used in make-ready as adjustments are made. The fact that the material is being pulled over such a long distance between units can make register difficult on lightweight materials.

STACK PRESSES

The stack press uses less floor space by placing units above one another. While gaining productivity in terms of floor space, the ease of operation is reduced. On manually controlled presses, the operator must climb up to make adjustments on the units above the floor. Modern remote-control devices reduce this factor; however, changing plate cylinders and aniloxes is still considerably less convenient. In principle, the stack press is simply an in-line where the web travels up through half the units and down through the rest. The disadvantages mentioned with in-line presses are therefore about the same for stack machines. Most stack presses are found in the wide-web applications, although there are a few narrow-web label stack presses on the market. Narrow-web stack presses are normally small enough to be operated from floor level.

COMMON IMPRESSION (CI) PRESSES

The common or central impression press was made popular by printing applications on lightweight films. First in printing cellophane and later with the development of polyethylene, the CI press virtually eliminated the problem of registration in multicolor printing. This was one of the biggest influences on the growth and improvement of the flexographic process. Since then the CI press has become the favored design for all wide-web applications, those over about 30 in. wide. In principle, once the web is positioned on the large common-impression cylinder, its like printing on a solid steel drum. Nothing moves. This makes top-quality possible, comparable to the best in any printing application. While the majority of CI presses are in the range of 36–60 in. wide, they are also manufactured as small as 7 in. and as large as 100 in.

The advantage of the CI is register, but the problem is making a single impression cylinder accurately in all dimensions. The quality of flexo print is limited by the accuracy of any single part of the impression system, anilox, plate, and impression cylinder. Only a small handful of manufacturers actually build the CI *drum*, as it is also called. The many CI press builders buy their impression cylinders from these sources.

There are *hybrid* presses that combine press designs on single machines. The most common hybrid combines the CI press with stack units located *downstream*. Figure 10-2 shows a very common configuration used in wide-web applications. The downstream units are frequently used for coating. There are often two clear coats applied in packaging. One is high gloss for scuff resistance and appearance. This coating is on the primary display surfaces of boxes and bags. The other coating is for non-skid purposes. Boxes and bags are stacked on pallets for handling and shipping. The surfaces that rest against each other are coated with a non-slip varnish to help prevent the products from slipping or sliding while being transported on conveyors or carried by fork lifts up ramps into tractor trailers and rail cars. Graphics can also be printed in these downstream units. The register tolerance, however, is not as tight as the registration of the units on the central impression cylinder.

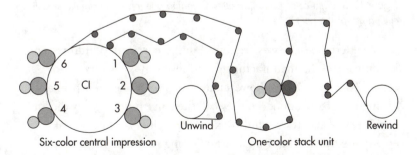

Figure 10-2. Common configuration of a CI press used in wide-web applications.

Since much of a press is dedicated to web handling, drying and converting, it is not unusual to find presses with enough print stations to permit running jobs with some stations while the others are being set up for the next job. The eight-color press in Figure 10-3 is an excellent example. While running a four-color job with two varnishes (on the stack units), the other four units may be prepared for the next job to be printed. As soon as the current run is complete, its four units are disengaged and the other four are engaged. Stock is changed for the new order which runs the same varnishes, and the production starts. A change-over crew washes the first four stations, and prepares them for the next run. This productivity is like having an additional press without taking all the space with two machines. The web handling, viewing, drying, and other converting requirements need not be duplicated.

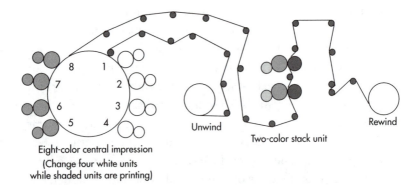

Eight-color central impression
(Change four white units
while shaded units are printing)

Figure 10-3. Eight-color press that allows running one job while simultaneously setting up for the next.

Sheetfed flexo presses are found in the corrugated industry and in some envelope manufacturing businesses. Box makers seldom refer to their machines, however, as "presses." Since their primary business is box production, they call their machines "rotary diecutters," "printer/slotters," and "flexo folder/gluers." During makeready the units are moved apart, allowing room for the operator to change plates and perform cleanup tasks. To run, the units are closed up and the board is fed through the machine, which prints and converts in a single pass. Jobs may be run through a second time when the number of colors requires. This is generally quite different from other sheetfed printing processes because there is no precise registration system. Designs must be very carefully planned and prepared if they require multiple passes through the printer. Register of print to cut and crease/score must also allow for more tolerance compared to common specifications used in folding carton production.

There are new, enhanced-graphics corrugated printing presses being used that are more like the sheetfed folding carton systems. These have units with space between to allow viewing and access to plates and aniloxes. More importantly, these machines provide space for drying after each color, which greatly improves the print quality and capability. Products printed on these machines may be diecut in-line. However, it is more common for the printed sheets to be converted off-line on flatbed diecutters and folded and glued on separate machines. These systems are very expensive in comparison to the standard corrugated printing and converting machines, and require different selling and pricing practices. Figure 10-4 shows one example of a modern corrugated press capable of pro-

Figure 10-4. A modern corrugated press. Photo courtesy of the Bobst Group.

ducing quality that rivals web printing. Such machines are dramatically changing the look of many corrugated converting plants.

WEB PRESS COMPONENT SYSTEMS

UNWIND AND TENSION CONTROL

Unwind stands consist of an expandable shaft to hold the roll of substrate and a means to control tension. Narrow-web presses generally accept 3-in. cores and rolls up to 30–36 in. in diameter. Wide-web presses often unwind rolls much larger, especially when printing heavy paperboard substrates. The tension control allows the operator to apply breaking to the roll to ensure it stops without coasting when the press stops and to make sure the web is under control as it enters the first print station. If too much tension is applied, the web might stretch. This is very critical when unwinding lightweight film substrates. Tension systems for paperboard are heavier than those for thin films. Figure 10-5 shows the unwind stations for a narrow-web and a wide-web press.

Between the unwind and the first print station there is often a web guide to accurately maintain the position of the web as it enters the press. This is critical for delivering product that has to be further processed after printing. If labels or film to be made into bags were not consistently positioned on the web the automatic processing of the printed material would be very troublesome if not impossible. Web guides consist of two electric eyes that sense the edge and make fine adjustments, steering the web continuously to keep the edge between the eyes.

Tension control is taken over in the press by a pair of *nip rolls*— rolls that pull the web. There is normally a nip roll just before the first print station, which pulls the web from the unwind. The next nip roll is after the last print station, often at the end of the press. It controls the tension through the printing and converting stations, if the press is so equipped. Tension is controlled in the rewind by a third tension zone. This zone is adjusted by increasing or decreasing the pull from the rewind shaft. This tension must be continuously monitored since the size and weight of this roll is changing continuously throughout the run. Excess tension in the rewind can contribute to blocking, or substrate sticking to itself. Blocking is influenced by several factors, tension being only one. Figure 10-6 diagrams the entire press, showing the three basic tension zones.

IMPRESSION

The press achieves impression in each of the print stations. The print station has controls to advance and retard the print position along the web.

Figure 10-5. The unwind stations for narrow- (top) and wide-web (bottom) presses.

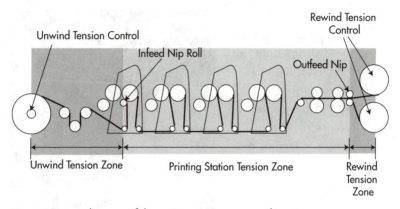

Figure 10-6. A diagram of the entire printing press and tension zones.

It also has controls to move the image from side to side. These are the controls that account for register. With few exceptions, angle is not adjustable on flexo presses. Squareness is determined by mounting the plates perfectly straight with the axis of the plate cylinder. The print station also has adjustments for both the plate-to-substrate impression and the pressure between the anilox roll and the plate. On many presses these two adjustments are not independent. This means that changing one affects the other. In such cases it is very important for operators to be extremely critical of their impression adjustments to obtain top-quality print. Figure 10-7 shows two impression systems. Close examination will show that the one on the top permits adjustment of impression without affecting anilox pressure. An increase in impression on the bottom one will result in increased anilox pressure to the plate, which must then be reset to avoid excess anilox pressure and overinking of the plate. This latter issue is important to understand when you consider the possibility of a slight difference in gauge or in surface uniformity of substrate after a roll change. The rougher the surface the more impression required for solid uniformity.

The ideal impression of plate to substrate is the least needed to achieve solid uniformity and mottle-free screens. The anilox roll should impress the plate just enough to print the entire surface of the plate. Remember: there is variability in every element of the

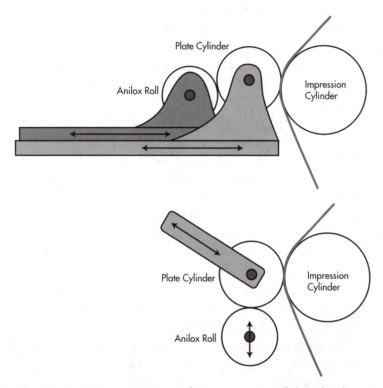

Figure 10-7. Two impression systems. Close examination will show that the one on the top permits adjustment of impression without affecting anilox pressure. An increase on the bottom system will result in increased anilox pressure to the plate, which must then be reset to avoid excess pressure and overinking of the plate.

printing system. Plate, stickyback, and plate cylinder tolerances are critical. Just a half a thousandth of an inch variance in each component totals one and a half thousandths in the system plus the tolerance in the impression cylinder and the substrate itself. When viewed as a system, top-quality printing requires the utmost attention to detail by all participants in the process.

DRYING SYSTEM

Most flexo presses are equipped with dryers or curing units. Dryers are either hot air or infrared. Ultraviolet (UV) or electron-beam (EB) curing are required for radiation-cured inks and coatings. It is essential for the printed images and coatings to be thoroughly dry before being rewound at the end of the press. Any moisture or liquid remaining in the ink will work its way to the top of the printed area. This rewets the surface and causes *blocking*, material sticking together, in the rewind roll. Sheeted jobs must also be dry enough to prevent smearing or scuffing as they are immediately handled and packaged at the end of the machine. With solvent- and water-based inks, drying is an evaporation or combined absorption-evaporation process. Heat aids drying because it increases the rate of vaporization of liquids. The vapors must be instantly removed from the drying area to keep the process going.

Infrared (IR) dryers are most commonly used with water-based inks on narrow-web presses. Of course they can and are used on all styles of presses where needed. IR dryers are very compact and relatively simple compared to hot-air dryers. IR is heat and thus the dwell time (time inside the dryer) must not be long or it will adversely affect the web, changing its size, register, and other end-use properties. IR is generally not the best for lightweight film substrates that shrink when heated. The temperature of the IR dryer is adjusted by the operator for job requirements.

Hot-air dryers are powered by either gas or electricity. The key to their effectiveness is in moving volumes of warm, dry air over the printed surface to rapidly remove the evaporating solvent, or amines and water vapor, in the case of water-based inks. Wide web presses are generally equipped with hot-air systems. Fast moving webs create an air barrier over their surface. This boundary layer must be penetrated by air from the dryer to achieve optimum drying efficiency. The air delivery systems in these dryers are, therefore, very important to their performance. The hot-air dryer elevates the temperature of the web, which speeds vaporization and provides high, focused air pressure through the boundary layer with low pressure above. This low pressure immediately exhausts the solvent-laden air up the stack. Since solvents contain VOCs, volatile organic compounds, it is normally necessary to capture these so they don't escape into the atmosphere. They may be recovered for reuse, called *solvent recovery,* or incinerated to accomplish this environmental objective.

The drying components on the press are really only part of the total drying system. The ink itself is possibly the most critical component. The right amount of solvent to maintain viscosity and transfer properties must also permit running speeds fast enough to achieve profitable production. Inks formulated to dry slowly will print easily at slow speeds but not allow complete drying at production speeds. These are the inks that students and new trainees like, since people work very slowly as they are learning new procedures. Inks formulated to print and dry at high speeds must contain a minimum of solvent to be removed in the drying process. These inks usually dry on the plates during slow makeready speeds but perform very well when running fast. Thin ink films are essential for high-quality printing and top press speeds. The more solids, that is pigments and resins, and the less diluent/liquid, the better the system.

RADIATION-CURING INK SYSTEMS

There are two approaches under the umbrella of radiation curing. They are ultraviolet and electron beam. Due to the costs of equipment, EB is generally found in very high-volume, high-speed production. While generally accepted as the superior technological solution, costs have limited its widespread use.

UV, on the other hand, is widely used and gaining in popularity. UV inks are really liquid polymers. The inks contain pigments, resins that are acrylic prepolymers before curing, acrylic monomers to control the viscosity, photoinitiators, and additives. UV inks, photosensitive polymers, are chemically cross-linked when exposed to high-intensity UV radiation. The liquid is almost instantly changed to a solid. From the press operator's view, it is "dry." It can be converted, handled, and further processed without delay. While UV printing has been around for many years, it is still in a stage of development and no one knows just how far, or what directions might be taken as this technology becomes more widely used.

UV has many very desirable qualities in terms of the pressroom and flexographic printing. It has a number of issues that have been problematic as well. The motivations, however, are very strong to overcome these problems in order to take advantage of the benefits. The driving force for UV as a replacement for solvent systems is the virtual elimination of VOCs. This would remove the need for expensive solvent recovery or other emission control systems. To the printer, the most valuable aspect of UV printing is that the inks don't dry until exposed to the UV radiation. Therefore, all problems associated with drying rate like dirty printing, build up of dried ink around edges of images, drying-in of aniloxes, and constant washing of plates following brief stoppages are eliminated. Of course, if it doesn't dry, you don't have to wash up at night. This is a tremendous value to all who operate less than 24 hours a day.

The problems have been difficulties in achieving solids without pinholes on film substrates, excess heat buildup on the substrate, incomplete curing, and issues of odor retained in the product. The greatest potential benefits are to be realized in wide-web film applications, due to the elimination of solvents. Questions associated with uncured residuals have, however, wisely caused the industry to move with caution. The very high cost of installing curing units on these large presses will continue to make progress slow for the foreseeable future. The narrow-web label industry, on the other hand, has embraced UV flexo much more quickly due to its printing benefits and the more affordable solutions that are readily available from many competitors. This is the best area for printing process improvements that will benefit the wide web printers as they increase their use of this printing technology.

The last issue of importance is viscosity. The flexo inking system transfers relatively low-viscosity liquids very well. Early UV inks were much higher in viscosity, and performance on the press was not always ideal. New lower-viscosity inks seem to achieve better results. The UV radiation curing approach should continue to improve and gain market share.

IN-LINE CONVERTING

The press is a system with many interdependent functions (Figure 10-8). The obvious interactions include speed of the press and drying rate of the ink and dryers. One can't print faster than the inking system can perform. The converting units on the press, in general, come after printing functions. Converting capability often sets the pace for the entire system. For example, if converting speed on a narrow-web press cannot exceed 200 feet per minute, the entire printing system must be set up to perform at its best running 200 ft/min. This is not quite as simple as slowing the press. The inks and dryers are set up for print speed. The inks, therefore, must be tuned to stay open (print clean) at a slower speed. The time inside dryers may require adjustment of air and heat. Similar interactions exist between plate systems and substrate. The plate required to print on a porous substrate may transfer ink slightly differently from the plate normally run by a given printer. The ink transfer attributes of this

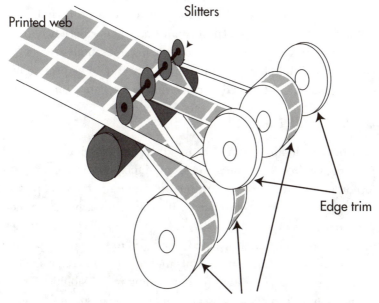

Figure 10-8. Schematic of the inline printing and converting process.

different plate necessitate special modifications to the ink and possibly even an anilox change.

Inline converting (as opposed to converting product off line or in a separate operation) is done to speed throughput and reduce costs associated with separate makereadies and materials handling. In-line converting activities, however, can cause problems in the printing units due to vibrations of the press drive system or the web itself. Imagine the effect of a repeated bumping as a sheeter impacts the web. This can cause a bump in the drive shaft which delivers power to every print station. This intermittent jolt can cause interruption of smooth drive to the print unit causing a slur—a band of dark or light print across screens and solids. Any action that intermittently impacts the web can also cause a quick move in the web itself. If the press cannot absorb that vibration or movement it will cary back to a print station, causing a slur. This points out the importance of precision tooling in the converting stations and excellent engineering of the converting units into the rest of the printing press. It also suggests that converting in-line is not always the way to go. Planners must have the experience to determine those times when the converting operations are not compatible with in-line printing. Those jobs should be printed in one operation and finished or converted in a separate one.

OTHER PRESS FUNCTIONS

Web viewing, in-line corona treating, turning the web for two-sided printing, laminating of other webs, and digital imprinting are just a few other operations commonly incorporated into the total printing press system. These are also part of the interactions and can affect the other parts of the total press system. Flexographic printing, by itself, is really quite easily learned compared to some other printing processes; however, the interactions that result from creative manufacturing solutions result in very demanding responsibilities. For the mechanically inclined who also enjoy problem solving activities, these jobs are very rewarding and always challenging.

11 EACH APPLICATION IS A SYSTEM

Any flexo production requires a specific system for best results. This system is composed of the substrate, inks, plates, anilox rolls, and graphics specifications. The substrate is most often the primary determiner of the operating flexographic printing system. Ink-film thickness is determined by the surface smoothness, absorbency and wetting properties, and the degree to which ink lays smoothly on it. The anilox roll controls wet ink-film thickness by the volume of ink in its cells. Volume of ink determines the capability of graphics reproduction. The more ink required to cover the substrate with density and uniformity, the more coarse the screen ruling (lines per inch) must be. If the customer is not satisfied with a 100-line-screen job, then a choice can be made to change to a smoother, less-absorbent substrate that will demand less ink (a thinner ink film).

While one medium-durometer (hardness) plate may perform satisfactorily on a range of surfaces, there is likely to be a best choice if the printer wants the highest-quality graphic reproduction possible. When substrate changes, this choice of plate material should also be re-optimized. Since plates combined with ink film and substrate determine tone reproduction curves (dot gain) all the prepress work must be tailored to this specific *reproduction system.*

If you follow the train of thought presented above, you are ready to think as you should about the logical process required to determine the specifications for a given operating flexographic printing system. There are simple tests that need to be run to learn the requirements of the systems if a printer needs to perform at the highest possible/affordable level.

"Highest possible" suggests optimum choices of each element in the system. This is an ideal approach, but often not one that is possible due to economics and other considerations. The best example to clarify this necessity for compromise is the corrugated printer who is required to print on three or four distinctly different substrates, not to mention the board flute patterns. At a cost of $15,000 to $30,000 per anilox and as much as several hours for anilox changes, optimization for specific surfaces is outside the window of economic practicality. Therefore, affordable, rather than highest possible, is often a real determiner of the ultimate capability of the total system. On the other hand, a flexible packaging producer may only print on one or two surfaces. In this case optimization is the only way to go, and is not the least bit impractical. Narrow-web printers using modern presses can optimize for many systems. The lower cost of small aniloxes along with the fast-change anilox systems on the presses make it possible to change rolls for each job. The top performers take advantage of these opportunities to compete at the highest quality levels on all customer-defined systems. To design the printing system, each converter must define the "common systems," as described above.

Once the substrate(s) is/are specified, a test image should be chosen or created. So many test images are available, there is little need to start from scratch. Some types of work, however, may have unique requirements that should certainly be included in the test targets. The standard elements are solids (areas large enough to compare to job demands), tone/dot gain scales in the appropriate range of screen rulings, impression targets, and positive and reverse lines and type of a range of weights. Figure 11-1 is an example of a typical test image. Whether done at the same time or later, calibrated register targets should be run to determine the register tolerances from station to station on the press.

Running the tests should start with planning. A test protocol with all the record keeping set up in advance will make the test pressrun go much faster. It will also help to avoid missing key elements that would have to be returned to later at considerable cost of machinery

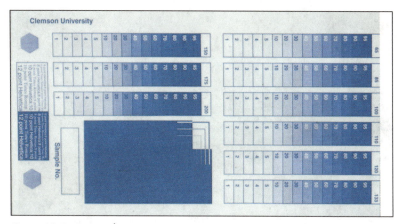

Figure 11-1. A typical printing test image.

and manpower. Where more than one substrate is to be run, each should be sequenced in order of smooth to rough so ink adjustments will not spoil the ink for the next substrate in the test. Samples should be flagged with detailed labels after the press has been allowed to run long enough to be stabilized. These labels should be made up in advance and in sequence to expedite the test.

Aniloxes may be used from the existing inventory. If optimization is the goal, it is common to conduct this process with a banded anilox roll designed specifically for the range of substrates being tested. Figure 11-2 is a banded anilox roll designed for flexible packaging applications. It has a series of engravings that vary both in cell count and volume. With one roll, a banded anilox allows running many tests simultaneously. It is important to note, when running banded rolls, there must be a compromise in the ink setup, which might mean that better results could be obtained in any given band if fine ink adjustments were tailored to that section of the anilox. Banded rolls are very valuable tools to expedite the optimization process and are widely used. Institutions doing service work for flexo printers often conduct banded roll testing to help their customers start their own testing closer to the final target.

Analysis of the test requires many readings with a densitometer, as well as visual observations. The first evaluation should be what I

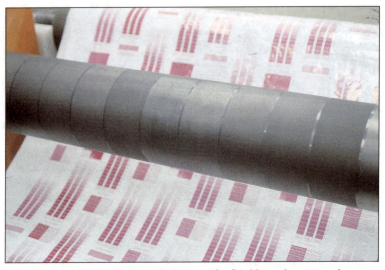

Figure 11-2. A banded anilox roll designed for flexible packaging applications.

call the "arm's-length test." Very simply, if the print looks bad, it is probably not worth taking many readings with instruments. "Looks bad" means dirty screens, poor solid uniformity, filled-in reverses, and pinholes or other voids. Figure 11-3 shows some examples of print that failed the "arm's-length test." The samples that look good visually will most likely be the ones that show the best instrument measurements. These samples must be read for solid ink density (SID) and dot percent, and they must be evaluated for solid uniformity. Solid uniformity considers freedom from mottle, pinholes, and other voids. The ideal print has clean screens with lowest possible dot gain and good SID. Of course, the more ink, the higher the SID. The more ink, the more dot gain. Therefore the best anilox choice is the one delivering the least amount of ink required to achieve necessary SID. Some printers choose an anilox that prints lower volume for less dot gain; however, in process printing this approach will seriously reduce the printable color gamut, the total range of colors. Low density yields less saturated colorsand, thus, is only adequate for soft images with pastels to highlights.

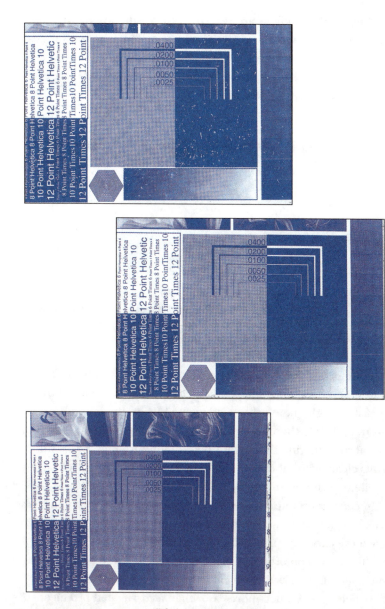

Figure 11-3. Some printing will fail the "arm's-length test," a good indicator that it will not pass the instrument measurement tests. (Top) Too little ink to cover dust particles and voids in substrate; (middle) clean solids, no voids, and open reverse type and lines; (bottom) too much ink filling in reverses and shadow end of scales.

After all the readings are recorded, the results are plotted and the decision is made on the optimum anilox for the given substrate. Figure 11-4 shows three dot gain and SID measures for printing on solid bleached sulfate (SBS) board, which is the workhorse in the production of folding cartons.

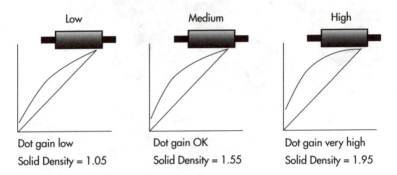

Low	Medium	High
Dot gain low	Dot gain OK	Dot gain very high
Solid Density = 1.05	Solid Density = 1.55	Solid Density = 1.95

Figure 11-4. Three dot gain and SID measures for printing on SBS board. It can easily be seen that the middle anilox roll meets the requirement of both density and low dot gain. The left anilox has less dot gain but SID is too low; the right scenario has excellent SID but dot gain is excessive.

If the printer must have one anilox to serve a variety of substrates then the choice will be different. The best anilox will transfer just enough ink to achieve adequate SID on the most absorbent substrate. It will, therefore, produce more dot gain than desired on the substrate having the highest ink holdout. As long as this still prints clean, without dots bridging or reverses filling in, good (not excellent) printing should be achievable.

In conclusion, the substrate and end-use specifications define the system by determining the anilox, plate, ink, and viscosity required to achieve excellent print. The more requirements put into the system, the more compromises that are necessary. Printers who do just one material, such as 6-, 12-, and 24-pack liquid carriers, can optimize their system much more easily than a corrugated producer required to print on different flute sizes and a variety of liners from high-holdout coated to bleached kraft. The narrow-web printer has a big advantage over its larger-format counterpart, because small presses permit virtually instant changes of aniloxes at roll costs that are more easily paid back. The printer who goes to the trouble to optimize his flexo systems can produce quality that will rival that of any printing process at very competitive costs. The printer who doesn't take the time to test and engineer his system will pay every day for his shortcuts, and always be vulnerable to competition from better printers. Knowledge is today's competitive edge.

12 In-Line Converting

F lexography's most competitive advantages with other printing processes are its variable repeat length and the variety of in-line converting operations that can be easily engineered with the printing units. This chapter explains the common converting operations. There are many specialized converting functions engineered in line with flexo and other printing operations. If it is more productive and profitable to convert the final product in-line, then it can be done. The decision to convert at the same time as printing is based on careful analysis of speeds and costs. The key to successful converting in-line is the ability to both print and convert at speeds that are both productive and compatible. If printing can be done at three or four times the speed of converting, it might be better to buy one printing press and three converting machines. This example is admittedly simplistic, but it is a basic consideration. Converting in-line also has major implications for labor and the skill required. Because in-line converting is achievable does not mean that it is the best way.

CONVERTING OPERATIONS

Converting simply means changing the form of the substrate from the way it was purchased into a different and more useful form. Since substrates are usually made in roll form, one of the most basic converting operations is sheeting, feeding the roll through a cutter of some sort and breaking it into precise lengths. Often this is combined with the next most common operation, slitting. Slitting simply breaks the web along its length, into multiple webs. Paper mills slit mill rolls into widths for common demands and, in turn, sheet them into customer order sizes for sheetfed printing or for further converting. Figure 12-1 shows how a flexo press can print any number of colors and deliver several rolls of finished product. Creative printers mix different customer orders in one production run and slit them into individual rolls at the same time.

Figure 12-1. A flexo press can print any number of colors and deliver several rolls of finished products.

Another very common converting operation is diecutting. Instead of putting a sheeter in the last position of a press, a special cutting die is installed. A cutting die converts the web or sheets into special shapes. Envelopes, paperboard cartons, tags, and labels are all cut to shapes as required by their final function. The cutting tool may be a rotary die or a flatbed die. Figure 12-2 diagrams these two common types of tooling.

Dies not only cut but crease, score, and perforate. Creasing and scoring are often used interchangeably; however, here we will define creasing as simply molding the material between male and female lines in the die resulting in a slightly weakened line, normally but not always straight. Scoring, on the other hand, is a partial cut into the substrate which creates a sharper fold or bend. While the sharp bend may look better, it is weaker, having cut part of the material and therefore is used cautiously for structural, strength reasons. Perforations are common in making "tear-off" tags and tickets. They are simply cuts that are intermittent, leaving enough uncut material to hold the product together until the perforated area is removed or torn off.

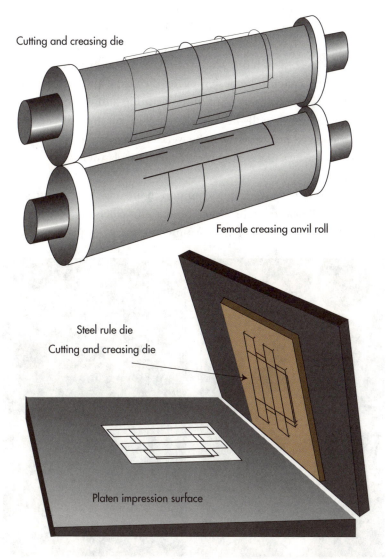

Figure 12-2. Two common types of diecutting tools, rotary (top) and flatbed (bottom).

Diecutting, slitting, and perforating may also be done entirely through the substrate or only through the face stock, in the case of pressure-sensitive materials. Most PS labels are face cut, slit, and perforated and the material between the labels is removed on the run. The ability to remove the waste on the fly is one of the greatest advantages of converting webs in-line. Figure 12-3 illustrates face cutting and waste rewinding. Sheetfed printers of PS labels have a labor-intensive task at hand when they have to remove the waste matrix, as it is called. The design of the die shape and its layout on the web are critical to successful in-line cutting and waste removal. Some shapes are virtually impossible to "strip" on the run because of the die shape or position on the web. Commercial diemakers are valuable resources in assisting the designer or planner to "design" a successful solution.

Laminating is another very common in-line manufacturing process. In the case of a producer of tags and labels, it is common to print and then laminate a clear film over the print just prior to

Figure 12-3. Face cutting (left) and waste rewinding (right).

diecutting. This produces a product impervious to moisture and protected from abrasion or from tampering. Laminating is often done for appearance, yielding a shiny, rich appearance compared to the product as it was printed alone. Laminating may be done in a number of ways. Sometimes a pressure-sensitive clear film or even

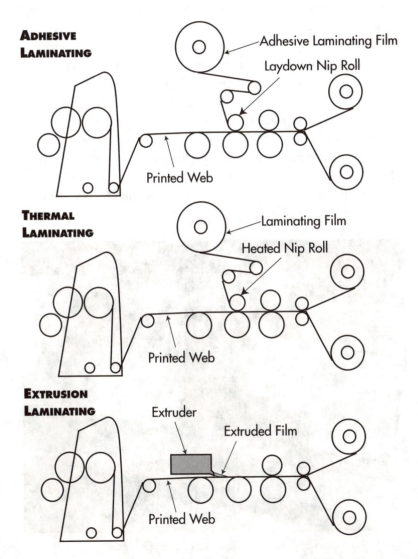

Figure 12-4. In-line laminating.

another printed web is simply adhered to the primary web. Another method is to apply an adhesive in the last printing station, or on a special in-line coater and then lay down the laminating web over this adhesive. In high-volume production an extruder can be positioned over the web and a film extruded directly onto the printed web. It is also possible to apply a film onto a web thermally, laying the film down, followed by passing the two materials through a heated nip. Figure 12-4 illustrates these in-line laminating concepts.

Forming, folding, and gluing are still more converting operations that are commonly performed in-line with printing. These are by no means limited to flexographic printing methods. Newspapers, sacks and bags, and boxes and cartons are all folded in line. Publications and paper or film substrates being converted into bags are folded in this way. Bags and boxes are glued by simply applying adhesive to the joint just before the two surfaces are joined. This glue application is achieved by rollers or by pneumatic (air) means as shown in Figure 12-5.

Figure 12-5. Rollers or pneumatic means are used to apply glue.

Converting knowledge and creativity can be the competitive edge. Narrow-web presses are really general printing and converting systems. They are offered in standard forms for use in the widest variety of applications. The press is capable of printing on both sides. It is equipped with die stations capable of cutting, creasing, and scoring the web. Many such presses have a laminating unwind and rewind, in addition to multiple rewind units for final product. Laminating unwinds can also be used to introduce another printed web or webs of many other materials, such as fabric or magnetic media. A conveyer can be attached to the last converting station to gather sheeted products. Many machines are converting devices first, and printing is inserted where and as needed to decorate the material before converting.

Very little product is simply printed. Most products must perform multiple functions, and printing is often secondary. Since marketing and communication are associated with most products, print becomes a critical part of the total scenario. Today's growth of flexographic printing is often driven first by its history of in-line converting and supported by the high-quality print achievements. Where there is high activity, there is economic incentive. Where there is market, there are opportunities. Success breeds success. Flexographers who are creative and enjoy challenges continue to be successful in competition with alternative printing processes. They should also be open to adoption of alternative printing processes, since these too are readily put in-line with flexo to improve the finished product.

13 TRENDS AND THE FUTURE

Talking about trends and especially the future is not far from "crystal ball gazing." It is fun to use evidence of the present to project the future, and writing it down surely results in fun for the reader, especially when it is being read at a time well into that same future. By that time (or is it this time for you?), the "book" may be history for the very same reasons. Change is continuous, the only certainty, and that is really what this chapter is about.

It is expected that flexo print quality will continue to improve. As evidenced by the awards program entries of the major trade and technical associations, this trend has continued on an upward course for many years, and this year showed no leveling off. This quality trend will continue to be supported by fin- tuning of plate, ink, anilox, and substrate technology along with creative and technological refinements in digital prepress.

Color strength and color control will be expected at higher and higher levels. Today color management systems are hot topics, and many software products are hitting the market. Limited experience combined with high hopes and great potential value cause the crystal ball to say "flexo will benefit greatly." The leaders will demonstrate to the rest that the scientific approach works and the process is very repeatable when treated as a total system. The customers will increasingly specify colors by the numbers resulting from spectral measurement. The designers and prepress producers will be calibrated, and rely on the numbers too. The printers will rely on their ink suppliers for colors by the numbers, and with thin ink films from ever more precise aniloxes, predictability and repeatability will be realized on press.

The same forces for consistency cause this forecast to also point at continued growth of UV applications in flexo printing. In principle, the 100% solids ink system, available in flexo-compatible viscosities, should make for easier achievement of repeatable color since varying amounts of volatiles are eliminated. This, of course, assumes the scientific and tightly controlled processing of the inks themselves as well as the tightly monitored and controlled printing process.

Given competitive quality and tight color tolerances, the versatility from variable print repeat and in-line converting at productive press speeds promises to keep flexo competitive with offset lithography into the foreseeable future. If true variable-repeat lithography were to be achieved, then the advantage of low-cost plates would introduce a significant new market force. Speaking of plate costs, it would seem that with more competitors constantly entering the market and with a continuing trend toward thinner plates, the costs of flexo plates would begin to decline.

In the long run this will be significant to the growth of the flexo process. In the larger applications gravure, always proclaimed as so costly due to cylinder preparation, is more competitive than many realize. Gravure should not be cast aside as a continuing competitor to flexo. It certainly remains as the most consistent-quality producer of all printing methods. It is too early to have more than a foggy crystal ball when it comes to digital. In large-format, short-run production, digital is certain to be a competitor to flexo, as it already is to screen printing. It is also not a question that digital units will be installed on traditional presses for variable information. These applications will help pay the developmental costs for continuously improved speed and quality. Before this book is retired its readers will have much more experience to build on.

Plates will continue to be thinner and work done in the '90s will lead to new approaches to the resilient layers under the plate. Sleeves will become the dominant plate cylinder approach in wide-web applications, reducing costs on short-run work needed in a "just-in-time" market. More plates will be imaged from digital drivers and less from film. The market will reduce the cost of this technology, which will, in turn, speed its popularity. It is likely that less-expensive digital plate imagers will be developed. The incentives are clearly significant.

The newspaper and advertising insert applications appear to have passed the experimental stage and, with more presses being installed, it is expected that this trend will continue on a slow but steady pace. The benefits of high-rub water-based inks and bright, high-density color sell. The crystal ball is far too fuzzy to suggest any other inroads into the publication market. There is opportunity here for the narrow-web flexo printer. We'll see if it is developed.

Folding cartons fall into a very different area where variable repeat and fast, in-line converting promise to continue the rapid growth that started in the mid '90s. Sophisticated press controls and easy provision for UV systems add to the appeal of flexo.

Direct-print corrugated promises to continue its growth in high-end enhanced graphics. The capability of the flexo process is proven. The paradigms of the box converters will fall away, as have those of many other segments. Those competitors that tool up for the niche markets will teach many others how to capitalize on their capability. They will have increasing competition from the litho label producers, and this is where costs will determine the ultimate mix of approaches.

Possibly with a few exceptions, revolutionary changes are not expected due to the capital in place and that required to implement major changes.

This is a good place to stop. There are enough predictions here already to provide years of teasing and embarrassment. Better to open our eyes and ears and report what really happens. I'm ready; are you?

GLOSSARY OF TERMS

ADDITIVE PRIMARIES In color theory, red, green, and blue light which together may be combined in various proportions to create new colors.

ADHESION The state in which two surfaces are held together by interfacial forces; measure of the strength with which one material sticks to another.

AM SCREEN Distinct from FM screen, the letters "AM" stand for "amplitude modulation," which in this case refers to the highlight to shadow areas of a halftone screened image being made up of halftone dots that vary in size.

ANALOG PROOF A proof that is made photographically from one or multiple negative or positive film images.

ANILOX ROLL Mechanically or laser-engraved metering roll used in flexo presses to meter a controlled film of ink from the fountain roller to the printing plates.

BASE Plate backing, usually a polyester sheet, which provides dimensional stability to the photopolymer flexographic plate.

BASIS WEIGHT The weight of 500 sheets (one ream) of any paper in its given basic size. Newsprint weights are based on a 24×36-in. sheet, other publication grades on a 25×38-in. sheet.

BCM Billion cubic microns per square inch, the most common specification for anilox roll cell volume.

BINDERY An area within a printing plant that carries out finishing operations (like cutting and folding) to printed material.

BLOCKING Substrate sticking to itself after being printed and rewound.

BRIGHTNESS A paper property, defined as the percentage reflection of 457-nm radiation.

CELL COUNT The number of cells per inch on an anilox roll.

CELL VOLUME The amount of ink an anilox cell can hold, specified or measured in billions of cubic microns.

CENTRAL-IMPRESSION-CYLINDER (CIC) PRESS A multicolor printing press that has one large impression cylinder surrounded by two or more plate cylinders.

CIELAB A color model based upon the standards developed by the Commission on Illumination, or in French, the Commission Internationale de l'Eclairage. The "L" stands for luminance and the "a" and "b" indicate the color's position on a coordinate system.

CMYK COLOR MODEL A color model based upon the subtractive primaries cyan, magenta, and yellow, as well as black. New colors are formed by combining cyan, magenta, yellow, and black in varying reflectance intensities. Black is used to provide increased darkness.

COEFFICIENT OF FRICTION (COF)   The ratio of the frictional force resisting movement of the surface being tested to the force applied normal to that surface (the weight of the material above that surface).

COLOR CORRECTION   A photographic, electronic, or manual process used to compensate for the characteristics of the process inks and of the color separation process.

COLOR MANAGEMENT SYSTEM   A means of maintaining accurate and predictable color throughout the reproduction process, including scanning, monitor display, color proofing, and process-color printing.

COLOR MODEL   A means of numerically describing colors within a system. There are several models commonly used in printing production including CIELAB, RGB, and CMYK.

COMPUTER-TO-PLATE (CTP) SYSTEM   System designed to image printing plates directly from computer data, therefore eliminating the need for film production and the use of contact plates.

CONTINUOUS-TONE IMAGE   An image that has a gradation of tones from light to dark, such as a photograph, watercolor painting, or charcoal drawing.

CURE   (1) Using high temperature to vulcanize the rubber of a plate or roller until the rubber reaches its optimum elasticity and tensile strength. (2) The crosslinking of molecules in UV and EB inks to change the material from liquid to solid.

DEMOUNT   Referring to a plate cylinder mounted on a shaft, having the bearing and gear journals.

DEPTH-TO-OPENING RATIO   The comparison of the depth of an anilox cell to the surface dimension of that cell.

DESKTOP PUBLISHING   A system comprising a microcomputer equipped with page-layout software and interfaced with an output device, such as a laser printer. This system allows the user to merge type and graphic elements in the creation of publications.

DIECUTTING   A finishing operation whereby some geometric shape is cut from the printed piece by pressing it against a flat, curved, or cylindrical surface with cutting and creasing edges.

DIGITAL PROOFING   Using a computer output device to create a facsimile image of how the printed piece will appear after printing on press.

DOCTOR BLADE   Thin, flexible steel, plastic, or composite blade that passes over a gravure plate, cylinder, or anilox roll, wiping off excess ink before an impression is made.

DOT GAIN   The change in apparent size of a printing dot from the film to the press sheet. Also referred to as tone value increase (TVI).

DUROMETER   A measure of rubber hardness usually made with Shore-A durometer gauge.

EFFLUX CUP   A simple viscometer such as the Zahn, Shell, DIN, or Hiccup; gauges viscosity readings rapidly in terms of the number of seconds required for the cup to empty through an orifice of known size.

ELECTROPLATING   The electrodeposition of an adherent metallic coating on an electrode for the purpose of securing a surface with properties or dimensions different from those of base metal. Used to apply hard chrome on conventional and electromechanical anilox rolls.

ENGRAVING A printing principle whereby an image area lies beneath the surface of a plate and the nonimage areas exist on the plate surface. Ink is applied to the plate and then wiped from the surface, leaving the ink in the recessed image areas. Pressure applied to the substrate transfers the image.

FACE The physical part of the flexographic printing plate that holds the image to be printed.

FLOOR The nonimage area of the flexographic printing plate.

FM SCREEN Stands for "frequency modulated screen," a halftone screen where the dots are of equal size and tones are created by varying the concentration of dots (highlight areas have sparse concentration of dots while shadow areas have dense concentration of dots).

GAMUT Range of colors rendered or described by a given color model.

GRAIN DIRECTION The alignment of cellulose fibers in a paper or paperboard substrate.

GRAY BALANCE The values for the yellow, magenta, and cyan that are needed to produce a neutral gray when printed at a normal density. When gray balance is achieved, the separations are said to have correct color balance. Gray balance is determined through the use of a gray balance chart.

GRAY LEVELS A term used to describe the number of individual tones that make up a digital halftone image.

HALFTONE A printed image of a continuous-tone original (like a photograph) that is composed of tiny dots to create the illusion of continuous-tone, though printed with one single density.

HALFTONE PHOTOGRAPHY The use of a process camera, contact screen, high-contrast film, and photographic chemistry to convert continuous-tone copy into halftone images.

HIGHLIGHTS The lightest areas in a reproduction.

HUE Quality of sensation according to which an observer is aware of differences of wavelength of radiant energy (color), such as blue, green, yellow, and red.

HUE ERROR The differences between an actual process color and the ideal theoretical color in its absorption and reflection properties.

IMAGE ASSEMBLY The phase of printing production that involves positioning pages or other layouts in the manner in which they will fall on the printing plate and subsequently on the press sheet.

IMAGE CARRIER The medium holding the inked image that prints it to a substrate; the plate.

INTEGRAL SHAFT A cylinder base design in which the supporting shaft is permanently attached to the printing cylinder.

LAMINATING A finishing operation that involves adhering one or more paper or film layers to a web or sheet to enhance visual and or performance properties.

LETTERPRESS A method of printing that uses a hard relief plate as an image carrier. The image area of the plate, raised above the nonprinting area, receives paste ink from rollers, and transfers it directly to the substrate being printed.

LIGHTNESS Perception by which white tones are distinguished from gray or black, and light from dark color tones.

LINE IMAGE A graphic composed of solid black and white areas only (with no other tones). Examples include pen and ink drawings and type characters.

Lithography A method of printing from a plane (flat) surface (as a smooth stone or metal plate) on which the image to be printed is water repellent and the non-printing area is water receptive.

Mandrel A shaft onto which demountable cylinders and sleeves are assembled; used for plate cylinders and anilox rolls.

Matrix A mold made from an engraving or type form, from which a rubber plate is subsequently made.

Matte Emulsion A textured surface of the film emulsion side, required for good drawdown while imaging sheet polymer plates.

Mechanical See *pasteup*.

Midtones or Middletones The tonal range between highlights and shadows.

Moiré An interference pattern caused by the out-of-register overlap of two or more regular halftone dot or line patterns. In process-color printing, screen angles are selected to minimize this pattern. If the angles are not correct, an objectionable effect may be produced.

Monomers A chemical combination of molecules corresponding to the individual units of a polymer.

Nip Line of contact between two rolls.

Opaquing The process of blocking out flaws in exposed negatives with some light-stopping material, usually applied with a brush or felt-like markers.

Overlay Proof A type of color proof made up of colored films that are imaged photographically with negative or positive films. Each color film is layered one on top of the next to form the proof.

Pasteup The historic method of page layout whereby paper-based type galleys and graphic elements are pasted into place on a stiff white board.

Pattern Plate The engraving or plates used for making the matrices, which are used to mold the rubber plate.

Photoinitiator An additive in ultraviolet curable inks and coatings that acts as a catalyst when the ink or coating is exposed to ultraviolet light.

Pick Resistance The ability of the surface of paper to resist the lifting of coating, film, or fibers from the surface of the substrate.

Pigment A component of ink, in particle form, that provides it with color.

Prepress A general phase of production that includes all operations taking place before presswork (like design, scanning, page layout, and platemaking).

Printing Technology associated with preparation and reproduction of images onto permanent substrates (like paper, plastics, and glass) in multiple copies.

Process Camera A large photographic device used to convert original hard-copy images (like photographs and paste-ups) to high-contrast film. The camera enables the operator to resize copy to exacting specifications.

Process Color The use of cyan, magenta, yellow, and black halftone images to create full-color printed reproductions.

Product Resistance The ability of a printed product, specifically package printing, to withstand exposure to chemicals and other volatile contents.

Proof A facsimile image of the final printed piece, created before presswork begins. Used for evaluation by production staff and customers of printing.

REGISTER   The fitting of two or more images on top of each other in exact alignment.

RELIEF   The dimension between the face and the floor of a flexographic or letterpress printing plate.

RELIEF DEPTH   The distance between the face and the floor of the flexographic printing plate.

RELIEF PRINTING   Printing that works on the principle of image areas raised above the nonimage areas of an image carrier. Paper is pressed against the surface of the inked image to transfer it.

RESILIENCE   The ability of the flexographic plate to rebound quickly after anilox contact and impression.

RESIN   A complex organic substance which, in solution, forms the varnish; after drying, resins are the binder, and film-forming materials.

REWINDING   The process of rewinding a roll of substrate to produce a proper size for the customer, to splice the ends together, and/or to remove defects.

RGB COLOR MODEL   Color model based on additive color theory; red, green, and blue light in various proportions are used to create new colors. Computer monitors display colors in RGB space using red, green, and blue phosphors.

ROTOGRAVURE   The printing process that involves the principle of engraving. An engraved cylinder is imersed in a fluid ink, the ink is wiped or doctored from the surface of the cylinder, and the ink left in the recessed areas of the cylinder is transferred to the substrate.

RUB   The durability attribute of an ink to withstand movement of printed surfaces against one another without being degraded.

SATURATION   The dimension of color that refers to a scale of perceptions representing a color's degree of departure from an achromatic color of the same brightness. The less gray a color contains, the more saturated it is.

SCREEN PRINTING   A printing process that employs stencils adhered to tightly drawn screens. Ink is forced through the openings in the stencil and onto the substrate. This process is well suited for printing materials like glass, wood, thick plastics, and textiles.

SHADOWS   The darkest areas in a reproduction.

SHARPNESS   The subjective impression of the density difference between two tones at their boundary.

SHOULDER   The physical part of the flexographic printing plate that lies between the image area and the non-image area.

SLEEVE   Tubular component that can be mounted on a mandrel; an alternative to an integral or one-piece cylinder.

SLIDE ANGLE   See *coefficient of friction.*

SLITTING   Cutting printed sheets or webs into two or more sections by means of cutting wheels on a press or rewinder.

SOLVENT   Liquid that dissolves a solid. In ink, the evaporation of solvent leaves the solids behind as an ink film on the substrate.

SOLVENT RECOVERY SYSTEM   A system designed to remove evaporated solvents from dryer exhaust air and the pressroom air, collecting the solvent for reuse.

STACK PRESS   Flexo press configuration in which two or more of the printing units are directly above one another.

STOCHASTIC   See *FM screen.*

SUBSTRATE   Literally means "the layer beneath," a term to describe any printing surface (paper, plastic, wood, glass, metal, etc.)

SUBTRACTIVE PRIMARIES   In color theory, the pigment colors cyan, magenta, and yellow, which when printed one on top another form the additive primaries red, green, and blue, and the gamut of attainable colors.

TACK   An ink property defined as the force required to split an ink film.

THUMBNAIL SKETCH   The first phase of a design, where the designer creates a series of sketches to brainstorm ideas.

TONE REPRODUCTION   A term that relates the density of every reproduced tone to the corresponding original density. This relationship is best described by the use of graphical techniques.

TRAPPING   The creation of a slight overlap between background and foreground colors to compensate for the inevitable misregister that occurs on lithographic presses. Also a term to describe how efficiently one ink film lays down and adheres to the preceding ink film when printing multiple colors.

UNSHARP MASKING   Typically, an electronic simulation of a photographic effect that enhances the sharpness of the reproduction.

VECTOR-BASED GRAPHIC   A type of computer graphic that is stored in computer memory as a series of geometric shapes, rather than as a bitmap.

VEHICLE   The fluid substance into which all other ink ingredients are suspended. They are specific to solvent-based, water-based, or radiation-curable ink systems.

VISCOSITY   A property of an ink defined as the resistance to flow, or simply the fluidity or thickness of the ink.

VISIBLE SPECTRUM   Portion of the electromagnetic spectrum that stimulates the light-sensitive cells of the human eye.

VULCANIZATION   The process in which gum is cured, changing its physical properties to rubber.

INDEX

About the Author

J. Page Crouch received both his bachelor's and master's degrees from San Diego State University, where he then taught for two years before beginning his doctoral work at the University of Missouri, Columbia. He joined the Clemson faculty in 1968, where he lead the development of the school's graphic communications program, supported by a strong and committed team. He has authored numerous articles on a wide variety of print and print education topics. He has served as a board member of the Flexographic Technical Association and the Foundation of the Flexographic Technical Association, and is a member of the Academy of Screen Printing Technology.

Crouch has been honored by the International Association of Printing House Craftsmen, National Association of Printers and Lithographers, International Publishing Management Association, Printing Industries of the Carolinas, Printing Industries Associations of Georgia, the Education Council of the Graphic Arts, Graphic Arts Sales Foundation, and by his peers at Clemson University. He has taught all the processes and has been active in most of the printing industry associations. Today he enjoys spending more of his time doing seminars and training programs on printing for education and industry.

ABOUT GATF

The Graphic Arts Technical Foundation is a nonprofit, scientific, technical, and educational organization dedicated to the advancement of the graphic communications industries worldwide. Its mission is to serve the field as the leading resource for technical information and services through research and education. GATF is a partner of the Printing Industries of America (PIA), the world's largest graphic arts trade association, and its regional affiliates.

For 76 years the Foundation has developed leading edge technologies and practices for printing. GATF's staff of researchers, educators, and technical specialists partner with nearly 14,000 corporate members in over 80 countries to help them maintain their competitive edge by increasing productivity, print quality, process control, and environmental compliance, and by implementing new techniques and technologies. Through conferences, satellite symposia, workshops, consulting, technical support, laboratory services, and publications, GATF strives to advance a global graphic communications community.

GATF*Press* publishes books on nearly every aspect of the field; learning modules (step-by-step instruction booklets); audiovisuals (CD-ROMs and videocassettes); and research and technology reports. It also publishes *GATFWorld,* a bimonthly magazine of technical articles, industry news, and reviews of specific products.

For detailed information about GATF products and services, please visit our website at *http://www.gatf.org* or write to us at 200 Deer Run Road, Sewickley, PA 15143-2600. Phone: 412/741-6860.

ABOUT PIA

In continuous operation since 1887 and headquartered in Alexandria, Virginia, Printing Industries of America, Inc. (PIA), is the world's largest graphic art trade association representing an industry with more than 1 million employees and $156 billion in sales annually. PIA promotes the interests of over 14,000 member companies. Companies become members in PIA by joining one of 31 regional affiliate organizations throughout the United States or by joining the Canadian Printing Industries Association. International companies outside North America may join PIA directly.

Printing Industries of America, Inc. is in the business of promoting programs, services, and an environment that helps its members operate profitably. Many of PIA's members are commercial printers, allied graphic arts firms such as electronic imaging companies, equipment manufacturers, and suppliers.

PIA has developed several special industry groups to meet the unique needs of specific market segments. Each special industry group provides members with current information on their specific market and helps members stay ahead of the competition. PIA's special industry groups are the Graphic Communications Association (GCA), Web Offset Association (WOA), Web Printing Association (WPA), Graphic Arts Marketing Information Service (GAMIS), International Thermographers Association (ITA), Label Printing Industries of America (LPIA), and Binding Industries of America International (BIA).

For more detailed information on PIA products and services, please visit our website *http://www.printing.org* or write to 100 Daingerfield Road, Alexandria, VA 22314 (phone: 703/519-8100).

GATF*Press*: SELECTED TITLES

Colophon

The second edition of the *Flexography Primer* was edited, designed, and printed at the Graphic Arts Technical Foundation, headquartered in Sewickley, Pennsylvania. The text was created by the author using Microsoft Word, then edited at GATF, and imported into QuarkXPress 4.0 on an Apple Power Macintosh. The primary fonts used for the interior of the book are New Baskerville and Futura. Line illustrations were drawn in Adobe Illustrator 8.01. Photographs were digitized on a Heidelberg Prepress Topaz scanner, and image editing and retouching to the digital files were done in Photoshop 5.5. Pages were proofed on a Xerox Regal color copier with Splash RIP.

Once the editorial/page layout process was completed, the images were transmitted to GATF's Center for Imaging Excellence, where all images were adjusted for the printing parameters of GATF's in-house printing department and proofed.

Next, the entire book was preflighted, digital imposed using DK&A INposition, and then output to a Barco Crescent 42 platesetter. The interior of the book was printed as 32-page signatures on a four-color Heidelberg Speedmaster model 102-4P sheetfed press, and the cover was printed four-up on a six-color Komori Lithrone 28 sheetfed press with aqueous coater. Finally, the book was sent to a trade bindery for perfect binding.